MARK B. MILLER

Baltimore TRANSITIONS

VIEWS OF AN
AMERICAN CITY
IN FLUX

REVISED AND EXPANDED

THE JOHNS HOPKINS UNIVERSITY PRESS | BALTIMORE AND LONDON

Originally published by Pridemark Press, Baltimore, Maryland, 1998
The Johns Hopkins University Press edition, 1999

9 8 7 6 5 4 3 2 1

The Johns Hopkins University Press
2715 North Charles Street
Baltimore, Maryland 21218–4363
www.press.jhu.edu

Library of Congress Cataloging-in-Publication Data will be found at the back of this book.
A catalog record for this book is available from the British Library.

ISBN 0-8018-6295-7

For My Daughter
JACQUELINE ANNETTE

AND

In Memory of My Parents
HARRIET MAKOVER MILLER

ERVIN MILLER

Aʟʟ ɪs ᴄʜᴀɴɢᴇ; ᴀʟʟ ʏɪᴇʟᴅs ɪᴛs ᴘʟᴀᴄᴇ ᴀɴᴅ ɢᴏᴇs.

EURIPIDES, *HERACLES* (C. 422 BC)

Tʜᴇ ᴡᴏʀʟᴅ ɪs ғʟᴇᴇᴛɪɴɢ; ᴀʟʟ ᴛʜɪɴɢs ᴘᴀss ᴀᴡᴀʏ;
ᴏʀ ɪs ɪᴛ ᴡᴇ ᴛʜᴀᴛ ᴘᴀss ᴀɴᴅ ᴛʜᴇʏ ᴛʜᴀᴛ sᴛᴀʏ?

LUCIAN (C. 120–200)

Wᴏʀʟᴅs ᴏɴ ᴡᴏʀʟᴅs ᴀʀᴇ ʀᴏʟʟɪɴɢ ᴇᴠᴇʀ
ғʀᴏᴍ ᴄʀᴇᴀᴛɪᴏɴ ᴛᴏ ᴅᴇᴄᴀʏ,
ʟɪᴋᴇ ᴛʜᴇ ʙᴜʙʙʟᴇs ᴏɴ ᴀ ʀɪᴠᴇʀ
sᴘᴀʀᴋʟɪɴɢ, ʙᴜʀsᴛɪɴɢ, ʙᴏʀɴᴇ ᴀᴡᴀʏ.

SHELLEY, *HELLAS* (1821)

FOREWORD

As a young *Sun* reporter in the late 1960s, I remember riding around the area known as Pigtown (which was then trying to make the transition from its common designation to the more refined Ridgely's Delight), with some members of the Urban Design Concept Team. This was a group of planners and architects, mostly from other places, that had been brought here to design the city's expressway system. The newcomers stared in awe at the marble steps and looming cornices. "A hundred years ago, this must have been quite a town," one of them said finally.

Indeed it was. It still is, although you have to look harder these days to prove it. Much of what the members of the Urban Design Concept Team admired in Baltimore thirty years ago has since disappeared, in part due to their own public improvements. Urban renewal—another huge federal program that began with good intentions, produced some benefits though at a high social cost, and was later discredited—also removed whole neighborhoods. Sometimes the new housing that was built on the sites has itself been demolished as uninhabitable in a mere thirty years.

Over more recent decades, the flight from the city of those with means, the upheavals caused by the shift from heavy to high-tech industry and a service economy, crime, and the partial breakdown of urban society, have made ghost towns of formerly viable commercial areas and residential communities. Yet for all that, the people who live here still believe in Baltimore and Mark Miller is clearly one of those people.

In *Baltimore Transitions*, he offers a mainly pictorial meditation, accompanied by his spare, lively, and sometimes eloquent prose, on the physical evolution of the city over roughly the past century. He does this via the tried-and-true method of combining historic and contemporary photographs of the same site and view. Miller both located the historic photographs and took the new ones, in some cases going to great lengths to achieve a similar vantage point. What does this time lapse photography of a city in process show us?

The photographs of Baltimore a hundred years ago reveal it to be a more-or-less physically homogenous city of two- and three-story rowhouses and five- and six-story commercial structures. The downtown streets are crowded with all sorts of businesses, stores, and theaters and thronged with human life. Steamships still lined the wharves along Pratt and Light Streets as late as 1925. And one cannot look at the 1930 photograph of the well-dressed crowds in the former central retail district at Howard and Lexington Streets without a twinge of nostalgia. As late as 1956, the cubist collage of rowhouse back buildings seen from the steeple of the First and Franklin Presbyterian Church on Park Avenue looks as if it was transplanted from Dickens's London. In the next picture, the rowhouses and back buildings have both disappeared, replaced by—what else?—a parking lot.

Generally, the current views suffer by comparison and we cannot help but wonder what all of our consultants' studies and high-priced planning efforts have gained us. Generally, the contemporary photographs show the emptying-out of the city and its ramifications as concrete expressway entrances and dull, windy spaces replace the former close-grained urban life.

The Inner Harbor is a good example as its historic functions of commerce and transportation gave way over the past 25 years to the more ritualized ones of shopping and eating. The most startling thing about the two views looking south over the Inner Harbor from the NationsBank Building is an arrogant intrusiveness of the IBM Building addition. Another pair of elevated views looking southeast from the Bromo Seltzer Tower, separated by three quarters of a century, illustrate the dramatic change in the appearance of the city and the transformation of its downtown from a tight cluster of multi-colored buildings of low elevation, housing a variety of small businesses, to a grid of monochromatic, widely-spaced high-rises, including some of exceeding banality, sheltering large agencies and corporations. Similarly, the author takes a rather dim view of the benefits to the average citizen of the Charles Center redevelopment.

In some outlying neighborhoods, the old buildings linger on with new uses. The local theater becomes the headquarters of the Salvation Army; the corner store selling general merchandise, a liquor outlet. In others, a Victorian mansard roof provides a welcome holdover from the streets' horse-and-buggy days amidst the other storefronts that have vigorously re-oriented themselves to the automobile.

Implicitly these photographs ask what Baltimore will look like a century from now. It is a cautionary question. Baltimore is a medium-sized city growing smaller, and its downtown cannot indefinitely accommodate more parking structures and boring office buildings—less noticeable in larger places such as New York, London, and Paris—without turning into a suburbanized version of itself. *Baltimore Transitions* will prove indispensable to city residents and urban planners alike as we grapple with the tough choices of the 21st century.

James D. Dilts
April 1998

Southwest Corner of Baltimore and Hanover Streets

1962

CONDEMNED: Baltimore and Hanover, once a thriving retail center, would soon fall for what became Charles Center South. As late as 1960, the Custom Shop, Turf Bar and Lounge, Bachman Tailoring, R.J. Toomey, Stein's Men's Clothing, Maryland Office Supply and Universal Clothing had lined the south side of Baltimore Street between Hanover and Liberty. They were gone by 1962, having either liquidated or relocated. The New York-based Custom Shop, a custom shirt outfit, opened in this 1890s-era building (center) in 1956. The venerable Hamburger's (far right) moved to its new store at Fayette and Charles Streets in 1963. *Pratt*

1998

RENEWED: By the late 1990s, Charles Center progeny like the Morris A. Mechanic Theater, George H. Fallon Federal Building and the Mercantile Safe and Trust Company stood as the "new-old" landmarks at Baltimore and Hanover. Its many design awards notwithstanding, Charles Center became the target of a certain school of "retro" critics advocating a return to street-level retail outlets and single-level streetscapes where cars and people mingled. Skywalks like the one spanning Baltimore Street, some claimed, alienated the various elements of downtown street life.

INTRODUCTION

Change, as they say, is constant, an ongoing process that never ceases, that waits for no one. It is also largely invisible: Buildings rise and buildings fall; streets get repaved, rerouted, graded and regraded; businesses turn over; ethnic/racial populations relocate; transportation technologies evolve; open space is filled with development; development is cleared for open space. We see and then we quickly forget, our memories of yesterday fogged by the concerns and rhythms of today. But through contrast, through viewing sets of old and contemporary photographs of the same view, our memories can be jogged, our sensibilities to change, sensitized.

Baltimore Transitions, like all then and now pictorials, is about seeing change through contrast, about documenting the obvious, though scarcely noticed and little appreciated. Our structural and social environment, Baltimore's in this case, is in constant flux, changing and evolving, profoundly in some places, subtly in others.

Structurally, the 300 block of N. Charles Street has changed little in 60 years, as a 1930s view of it here will attest. The well-scrubbed, recreational Pratt-Light waterfront of the mid-1990s, on the other hand, is almost unrecognizable from the gritty, industrial Pratt-Light waterfront of the early 20th century, a place of ratty wharves, banana boats and stevedores, not glass pavilions, Tall Ships and tourists.

What precipitates such change is varied and complex, and I've focused on some major influences here, mindful of the one question the reader might most often ask: How did things get to be the way they are?

Economic motivation triggered the harbor's metamorphosis, a process born in the early 1950s when a group of concerned, well-connected businessmen met to discuss urban decay and declining property values in the city's central business district. A half century earlier it was natural disaster, the great Baltimore fire of 1904 that, pun intended, ignited the sequence of events which ultimately led to the rebuilding of a new downtown. It was social and political reasons, racially-tinged housing policies specifically, that created in the 1950s high rise housing projects like Lafayette Courts; and it was social, moral and political reasons, civil rights legislation cum revisionist thinking, that tore them down.

Whether such change is good or bad, I've left it for the reader to decide. Change can be either, depending on one's perspective. It can also be both when one gives equal measure to form and function, aestheticism and pragmatism. The more "human" and intimate scale many preservationists admire in the city's late 18th and 19th century buildings and infrastructure—smaller buildings, narrower streets, streams that flowed openly—is offset by the congestion and population pressures that forced a dramatic change of scale and density throughout the 20th century.

Preston Gardens, a World War One era "city beautiful extravaganza," wrote author Carleton Jones, "took with it the terraced old warrens of Courtland Street, a whole hillside of elegant Federal architecture and domestic lore that was considered one of the most important neighborhoods in the country (politically and legally) in the decades before the Civil War." Preston Gardens also carpeted this legal district with a verdant oasis and unclogged its contiguous arteries to meet the pressing demands of automobile traffic. Charles Center, a mid-century-planned, award-winning urban renewal project destroyed the warm, intimate, cosmopolitan, urban busyness that had been the city's central business district. Charles Center also reduced traffic congestion and created underground parking space and open places for people to congregate.

Admittedly, I did not strive for total neutrality. Readers will, in places, notice my personal biases, my preservationist sentiments seeping through. I saw no point in even pretending

not to lament the tearing down of grand Victorian piles like the Rennert Hotel for drab (but aren't they all?) parking lots, or the downward spiral into war zones of once safe and structurally sound neighborhoods like Pimlico. Some change has no redeeming value, period. On the other hand, I distanced myself from that preservationist, lunatic fringe for whom form is all. Such folks never met an "old" building they didn't like, be it Colonial, Georgian, Federal, Greek Revival, Gothic Revival, what have you.

Other "historical" views cited here include the 1809 courthouse and Guy's Hotel when they graced Monument Square; the Mathieson Building when it dominated Baltimore's skyline; the 100 block of West Lexington Street before the transit mall; Jones Falls before the Fallsway; Waterloo Row before Waterloo Place; the harbor before Harborplace; Camden Yards before Oriole Park.

All views shown lie within the present political boundaries of Baltimore City and follow in rough sequence from the Inner Harbor out to the municipal suburban fringes. Whenever possible I shot the contemporary views from the same angle and distance as their historical counterparts. In some cases this was not possible, so radically had change swept across the manmade and "natural" landscape. Also, demolition, construction, and other instruments of change greatly altered some of these views soon after I shot them. At times, I developed a sense of incompleteness and an almost manic compulsion to "update" what can never be permanently updated, what is impervious to any final revision. Change is indeed the only constant, and "now" an illusion, a time and place fleeting as life itself—gone in the click of a camera shutter.

Baltimore TRANSITIONS

Views of an American City in Flux . . .

BALTIMORE FROM FEDERAL HILL
1752, 1850, 1876, 1901, 1933, 1958, 1966, 1995

Before Harborplace, the National Aquarium, the gleaming office towers and glass-walled skyscrapers. Before the Emerson Tower, Shot Tower, Power Plant, City Hall, The Basilica, Battle Monument, Washington Monument and the peculiar "courthouse on stilts." Before the paving of Pratt, Light, Calvert and Charles Streets. Before the Ericsson Line, Wilson Line, B C O Line, Old Bay Line and Old Bay. Before the paddle-wheel steamers and speedy clipper ships, the piers and wharves and the warren of waterfront warehouses. Before the great western loop of the Jones Falls was yanked eastward even, there was the town—inchoate and raw, hugging the harbor shoreline, moseying into its 23rd year.

A 21-year-old who could have used a few art lessons rendered it all in a flat, simplistic sketch. But what John Moale Jr., the would-be artist and son of one of the town's leading citizens lacked in artistic talent, he more than made up for in inspiration. Apparently, Moale had it that day in 1752 when he looked north from a barren bluff of red clay, later known as Federal Hill, and sketched what he saw, thus capturing the earliest harbor view of Baltimore extant and setting a precedent for others who took to the hill, sketch pad and/or camera in tow, and chronicled the city's growth as it expanded outward and upward from its original 60 acres around the harbor basin.

Moale drew his seminal portrait the same year that Dr. John Stevenson shipped an experimental cargo of flour to Ireland, thereby initiating the brisk trade that would turn Baltimore into a major seaport. Moale's sketch shows the calm before the storm, a town, excluding the nearby settlements of Fells Point and Jonestown, that claimed 25 houses, two taverns and a church. The latter was St. Paul's, shown at center, the first of what became four St. Paul's, all of them built on the original site. Just below it to the right is Edward Fottrell's house, Baltimore's first brick house with freestone corners that stood near the present site of the Battle Monument. The two-chimney, gambrel-roof building just to its right is Kaminsky's Tavern, a landmark until 1870. The harbor's shoreline extended further north in those days, lapping up to present day Water Street.

Extensive landfill projects beginning in the 1780s had reconfigured the harbor shoreline by the time photographers began shooting from the hill. The mid-19th century view shows a dense settlement (and highly combustible as Baltimoreans would learn a half century later) of waterfront warehouses and workers' homes built on a century's worth of landfill bulkheads. Most of Baltimore's well-to-do had long abandoned the hazardous, industrial harbor for the "heights" around Monument Square and Washington Monument (1829). Steeple of 1796 German Reformed Church (right) looks conspicuous against a skyline of few buildings exceeding four stories. Landmarks in 1876 view would dominate Baltimore's skyline for the next quarter century: Washington Monument, Basilica of the Assumption (1821) and City Hall (1875).

(Narrative continued on page 14)

BALTIMORE FROM FEDERAL HILL, 1901, *PEALE MUSEUM*

BALTIMORE FROM FEDERAL HILL, 1933, *PRATT*

BALTIMORE FROM FEDERAL HILL, 1958, *MARYLAND HISTORICAL SOCIETY*

BALTIMORE FROM FEDERAL HILL, 1966, *PRATT*

At the turn of the century skyscrapers, not monuments or churches, began to define the aesthetic of America's downtowns. Elisha Otis's electric elevators and the mass production of skeletal frame steel columns and beams made them possible. The William Le Baron Jenney-designed 10-story Home Insurance Company building, erected in Chicago between 1883–1885, was the nation's first. The 1901 view shows what many regard as Baltimore's first skyscraper—the newly-completed, Warfield-financed, 16-story Continental Trust Building, shown to the left of the 1889 U.S. Post Office. As buildings got taller, familiar landmarks like the onion-shaped towers of The Basilica, still visible in 1901 from Federal Hill, would fade from view. In foreground are early 19th century workers' homes that by 1930 would be replaced with factories.

The Great Fire of 1904 gutted Continental Trust and other turn-of-the-century buildings (Maryland Trust was another). Neverthe-less, they survived to shape Baltimore's skyline into the new century, remaining, along with the 1911 Muncie Building (just left of Tower Building, which is just left of City Hall), the big kids on the horizon until 1929, when they gave ground—or rather sky—to the 34-story Baltimore Trust Building (subsequently the O'Sullivan Building 1942–1949, Mathieson Building 1949–1962, Maryland National Building 1962–1994 and NationsBank Building 1994–); it remained the city's tallest building into the 1970s. To the left of Baltimore Trust in the 1933 view: 7 E. Redwood Street, B&O Building (1908) and Lord Baltimore Hotel (1928). The appropriately named 314-foot Tower Building, completed in 1912, originally headquartered Maryland Casualty.

Baltimore's mid-20th century skyline was nearly a mirror image of its Depression-era self. Indeed, the Inner Harbor during the 30 year period from the 1930s through the early 1960s seemed to wear a big DO NOT DISTURB sign. Nobody did. As early as

1930, investment in new commercial office space had dried up, decay set in and vacant warehouse and loft space reached 2,000,000 square feet. Said W. Burton Guy, past president of the Committee for Downtown: "In the grim days of the early 1950s Baltimore was like a sick old man, with no idea of what the chances of recovery were."

The sick old man's prognosis for recovery looked pretty good in 1966. Phase One of the Charles Center project, launched in 1959, was proceeding apace. The view here shows the George H. Fallon Federal Building (left) and Sun Life Insurance Building nearing completion. The April 1965 issue of *Progressive Architecture* had this to say about the city's emerging Inner Harbor renaissance: "This historic spot, its basin and its shoreline, can become the stage for a dramatic exercise in urban renewal. Now the scene of run-down docks and wharves and (with few exceptions) economically unsound business practices, Inner Harbor . . . emerges as a can-didate for the best use of water and open land in post-war U.S. urban renewal. Instead of cutting the water off from the city, as almost all our cities do, Baltimore—if this plan is followed—will thrust the living, 24-hours-a-day city into intimate and viva-cious contact with the harbor whence it sprang."

Enter the Greater Baltimore Committee's $260,000,000 Phase Two project. Launched in 1964, it turned the Inner Harbor into what the American Institute of Architects called "a masterpiece of planning and execution that took a ramshackle, rat-infested, crumbling old dock and transformed it into one of the most beautiful, humane, diverse center-city places in the world." The Harborplace pavilions, arriving in 1980, represented the Inner Harbor Renaissance in full flower. Built by the Rouse Company, they became the centerpiece for an Inner Harbor that began in the mid-1970s to explode with new skyscrapers and office towers:

A. Charles Center South (1975); B. USF&G (1974, sold to
Legg Mason, June 1997); C. 1st National Bank Building (1972);
D. 100 E. Pratt Street (1984); E. Legg Mason Tower (1989);
F. Commerce Place (1991, became Alex. Brown Building in 1997);
G. World Trade Center (1977).

Inner Harbor real estate took a beating during the post-Gulf
War recession, then rebounded and enjoyed a mini-renaissance
in the late 1990s. Vacancy rates for Class A buildings stood
at around five percent, and their owners were getting top dollar
for them: IBM sold the 28-story 100 E. Pratt Street tower to a
Boston real estate company for $137 million; Yarmouth Group
Inc., a New York pension fund consultant that paid $32 million for
250 W. Pratt Street in recession-ridden 1994, was asking $55
million for it in October 1997. Should the good times last, new
harbor office towers will no doubt spring up in the years to
come, adding density to the city's skyline but not height. Strato-
spheric skyscrapers on the order of the Sears Tower, Empire
State Building or New York's World Trade Center probably won't
sell here. Recall the outcry over the proposed 48-story Wyndham
Hotel at Inner Harbor East. Now that Baltimoreans have their
harbor back, they don't want it lost in the long shadows cast by
architectural Godzillas. This is Baltimore after all, not Chicago
or New York.

"An unhealthy looking tumour . . ." Minus the wooden signal tower and houses, this is the Federal Hill from which Mr. Moale sketched a century earlier. Baltimoreans in 1788 held a grand soiree here in celebration of Maryland's ratification of the Federal Constitution; thus the name Federal Hill. An enterprising sea captain in 1797 erected the wooden tower. Using a telescope and flags, he could alert harbor personnel of arrivals before the docksiders could. The tower was still in use in the 1830s, a time when other enterprising citizens were establishing shipyards around the hill. But Dr. Thomas H. Buckler was thinking landfill, not private enterprise, when he urged the city council in 1859 to shove the whole damn thing into the harbor basin, which he considered a public health hazard. Benjamin Latrobe Jr., under Buckler's private hire to engineer the project, echoed Buckler's sentiments, calling the hill "an unhealthy looking tumour upon the lower limb of the city, covered with mean dwellings and unsavory manufactories." The project was scuttled, thanks to an unaffordable $750,000 price tag and the stiff resistance of Light Street property owners. *Peale Museum*

Had Dr. Buckler had his way, General Benjamin F. Butler, Union commander assigned to Baltimore during the Civil War, would have been deprived of what became a union fort. Mindful of Baltimore's southern sympathies, Butler trained some 50 artillery pieces on the city, ordering his artillery commander on 31 May 1861 (almost six weeks after the April 19th riots on Pratt Street) to, if attacked, "open up on Monument Square with your mortars." The war delayed what had been proposed back in 1853: Fashioning the hill into a public park. Through city ordinance, it became one in 1875, and thus began the process of landscaping what was once an eyesore into the neat, mani-cured plateau pictured here. At left is the 27-story, 249-unit 100 Harbor View condominium, the "grande dame of South Baltimore," as some called it when it opened in 1993 on what had been the site of Bethlehem Steel's Key Highway ship building plant. Harbor View was the first edition of what developers Richard Swirnow and Parkway Holdings Ltd. hoped would be a new era for the Key Highway waterfront. With its units priced from $161,000–$1.7 million, it was a bold gamble in light of the modest sales of similarly priced Baltimore high-rise condos.

LIGHT STREET

GRITTY CITY: The Inner Harbor through World War Two was a place where smokestacks belched, men and women toiled and perspired and vermin scurried about the piers and docks. Tourists were almost non-existent, save for onlookers and hangers-on enamored with ships and energized by dockside bustle and the smell of fresh bananas. There was a certain excitement and no-nonsense, unpretentious quality to this place that can't be denied. Excursion steamboats like the ones pictured here docked at Light Street would be a familiar sight for another 40 years. The *City of Richmond*, one of the last of the excursion steamers to cruise the Chesapeake, operated through the early 1960s. The venerable Baltimore Steam Packet Company, better known as the "The Old Bay Line" (note pier with tower at right), had been hauling passengers and freight between Baltimore and Norfolk since 1817. *Maryland Historical Society*

PRETTY CITY: By the time the "Old Bay Line" made its last run to Norfolk in 1962, recreation and tourism, not commerce and steam, were propelling the Inner Harbor into a new era. It would be another decade before extensive landfill reshaped and restructured the basin shoreline and 10 more years before the Rouse-developed glass pavilions of Harborplace appeared (modeled after Boston's Faneuil Hall Marketplace, Rouse's first downtown "festival" market restoration project) appeared and Baltimore showed up on the cover of *Time*, toasted as the very model of a modern major port city. Some critics had feared the proposed pavilions would destroy the harbor's "openness." Others called the Cambridge Seven-designed 1981 National Aquarium (far right) a "fish tank" the city didn't need. All ate crow. Harborplace drew an average of 15 million visitors (the National Aquarium drew more than one million alone) per year, pumping millions into the local economy. New tenants, including the trendy Planet Hollywood, moved into the pavilions following a Rouse-financed (the company failed in its bid to win $13 million in public subsidies) spring 1998 overhaul. The author snapped this view from a fourth floor balcony in one of the first buildings completed at Inner Harbor West, the Christ Church Apartments (1974) for the elderly.

BEHIND THE WATERFRONT: Although a widened, post-1904 Light Street allowed for greater traffic flow, Baltimoreans were still isolated from their harbor. The piers, which made street-level, waterfront views hard to come by, created not only a physical barrier but a psychological one: Citizens removed from waterfront business could readily forget that Baltimore was a major seaport. The buildings at right housed produce companies like Tamburo Brothers, T.H. Evans, Joseph Lenhoff & Son, Snyder & Blankfard and Schley Brothers. Merchant's Barber Shop and Dangelo's Cafe served dock workers and shipping personnel. The Baltimore-Philadelphia steamers (note pier at left) were the first vessels of their kind to appear at Pratt and Light Streets, making their harbor debut in 1813. *Maryland Historical Society*

ON THE WATERFRONT: Light Street became a waterfront boulevard that encouraged Baltimoreans to reach out and touch their harbor. The new development allowed for unobstructed, panoramic views and easy access to harbor attractions like the 1976 Maryland Science Center (center). Opened in 1986, the Harbor Court condo, hotel and office complex (right) a decade later was operating in the black and claimed for its hotel a celebrity guest list that included Luciano Pavarotti, Robin Williams, Sharon Stone and David Letterman. 100 Harbor View (left) struggled on into the late 1990s with sluggish sales. Yet, its owners still had plans for a second, less lofty tower and other development, no consolation to some Federal Hill residents put off by its conspicuous verticality, its perceived mix of altitude and attitude. It "sticks out from a low-rise neighborhood like a sore digit . . . it is an earlier example of a headstrong mayor pushing a development against the advice of his professional staff," wrote one resident in a late 1997 *Sunpapers* editorial. The "grande dame of South Baltimore" plays to mixed reviews. To some, it's a grande place to live; to others, a grande symbol of gentrification run amok.

PRATT AND LIGHT STREETS LOOKING WEST, CIRCA 1900

RUSH HOUR FROM HELL: A classic photo often erroneously dated 1906 or later, it should encourage commuters who become unglued while stuck in bumper-to-bumper JFX or Beltway traffic to count their blessings. Before the widening of Pratt and Light in 1905, streetcars, horses, the B&O Railroad and later automobiles all competed for the right-of-way on Pratt Street. Little wonder that Pratt and Light remained for over 50 years the most congested point in Baltimore. The circa 1800 row of warehouses along the Light Street wharf exhibited the kind of exquisite symmetry found in once fashionable residential architecture like Pascault Row on Lexington Street. The only waterfront warehouses of their design to survive the fire, they were demolished for the widening of Light Street. Up until the early 1950s, when the city dismantled the piers, erected Sam Smith Park and extended Calvert Street south on landfill, the harbor basin's water line extended up to the present intersection of Pratt and Light. Steam dredging machines in the 19th century had deepened the channel basin so large ships could dock there. *Peale Museum*

Baltimore
TRANSITIONS

PRATT AND LIGHT STREETS
LOOKING WEST, 1994

LUNCH HOUR FROM 100 EAST PRATT STREET:
The author caught a free-flowing, liberated Pratt and Light around noon from the 100 East Pratt building's gravel-surfaced roof. Rush hour here can still cause horns to beep and blood pressure to rise, but at least the horses and trains are gone. Commerce and industry thrived here through the 1940s, then declined as water trucking began to cut into the steamboat transport industry and business moved further down the Patapsco. Inner Harbor redevelopment of the Pratt-Light waterfront included an ambitious landfill bulkhead project that in 1970 added 100 feet of rock and granite landfill to the western shore-line. Brick promenade at southeast corner of Pratt and Light, an area under water in the earlier view, was completed in 1972. The RTKL-designed C&P Telephone Building (1977) at southwest corner occupies former site of the National Biscuit Company. The $50 million, 1979 Baltimore Convention Center seen just west of it further boosted Baltimore's status as a tourist city and became the catalyst for a hotel-building boom. Convention Center construction took off nationwide after 1970, a time when only 15 cities could accommodate trade shows of 20,000 people. Fifteen years later, 150 cities could.

LOOKING SOUTH FROM BALTIMORE TRUST BUILDING, 1934

(Narrative follows)

LOOKING SOUTH FROM . . .

BALTIMORE TRUST BUILDING, 1934 *(Left)*

On a clear day . . . The legendary A. Aubrey Bodine might have captured this harbor view once afforded office personnel (and tourists on the observation deck 34 stories up) ensconced on the top floors of Baltimore's only art deco skyscraper. The ships sailing in and out, the stevedores loading and unloading cargo over the scruffy piers and docks, the trucks hauling produce along Pratt and Light, made for an impressive sight. Bethlehem Steel's floating drydock, an important ship repair center during World War Two, can be seen just left of Federal Hill Park. The circa 1905–06 factory and warehouse buildings along the north side of Pratt Street (below) between Light and Commerce housed manufacturing companies like Gray Marine Motor, Kessler Shoes, James A. Moor Elevators, Morton Coffee, Baltimore Seed and Norwood Sails. The fragrance of Old Bay and other spices pumped from the 1921 McCormick spice factory (far right, center) was an olfactory delight to generations of Baltimoreans passing through the harbor area during the summer months. Shown in distance are Federal Hill, South Baltimore and the middle branch of the Patapsco, with Brooklyn, Curtis Bay and perhaps even the northern fringes of Anne Arundel County beyond. *Maryland Historical Society*

NATIONSBANK BUILDING, 1995 *(Right)*

The harbor of heavy ship traffic and bustling port activity passed on long before office towers like 100 East Pratt Street spoiled full bird's-eye views of the harbor basin. The harbor's dramatic dowdy to chic metamorphosis began in the 1950s and gained momentum during the nascent years of Charles Center. J. Jefferson Miller, James W. Rouse, David A. Wallace and Martin L. Millspaugh—that dynamic foursome that guided the Charles Center project—turned their attention to developing the Inner Harbor for recreational and cultural use. Voters passed a $14 million bond issue in 1966 and Uncle Sam pitched in over $17 million in 1967; ground was broken a few years later. Shown from left to right: the I.M. Pei-designed World Trade Center, Legg Mason Tower, 100 East Pratt Street, USF&G (acquired by Legg Mason in 1997) Tower. The pricy homes ($140,000–$400,000-plus) in the 29-story, mid-1980s Harbor Court Condominium Tower (just left of USF&G Tower), developed by David Murdock, underscored the prestigiousness of harbor living on what was once blue-collar turf. Harbor View is shown on the site of Bethlehem Steel's old shipbuilding plant, which closed in 1983. Not much of the pre-renaissance Inner Harbor remains here including, sadly, for those old enough to remember, the pungent presence of McCormick Spice. The company had moved to Hunt Valley a few years before preservationists lost their battle to save the old factory. In 1989 it was torn down along with another part of the complex, Charles Carson's Marburg Brothers warehouse.

LOOKING EAST FROM . . .

400 BLOCK OF PRATT STREET, CIRCA 1915

Horsepower, the original kind, still hauled cargo from the piers along Pratt Street in the mid-teens. The block shown here housed through the years long-forgotten companies like C.C. Carver, U.S. Electrical Motors, Goeb-Mervis printers, L. Hilpert engravers, Pyrene Distributors, A.E. Sattler. The 12-story Candler Building, shown east of Frey's, was a monument of sorts to the city's efforts to attract big business, in this case Coca-Cola. Asa G. Candler was founder of the Atlanta-based Coca-Cola Co., and the building bearing his name, completed about 1911, was one of the soft drink company's three primary offices. After its sale in 1960, it served as corporate headquarters for Joseph A. Bank Clothiers. *University of Maryland Baltimore County*

1915

1997

400 BLOCK OF PRATT STREET, 1997

The Inner Harbor development of the 1970s widened Pratt Street and swept away all but the Candler Building and Power Plant, hidden by piers in the 1915 view. Built in 1895–1901 to supply energy for streetcars, the Power Plant by late 1995 had become an empty city landmark that no one wanted. In early 1997 the highly successful, Baltimore-based Cordish Company began developing it as a family entertainment emporium dubbed Metropolis at the Power Plant. Cordish had a formidable task: Six Flaggs Corporation in the 1980s had tried several entertainment formats at Power Plant before finally giving up. Cordish's first tenant, Hard Rock Cafe, drew patrons in droves when it first opened in July 1997. The McCarty-model guitar (Hard Rock Cafes in other cities use either Gibson or Fender models for their built-to-scale, neon guitar logos) shown in front gives new meaning to the term *heavy metal*; it measures 68-feet high and weighs over 3,000 pounds. The Candler Building, a decade after its $20 million renovation, was recovering from vacancy malaise, an affliction that had plagued other harbor real estate through the mid-1990s. In 1997 things were also looking up, literally, for the 1981, 11-story 400 East Pratt Street Building (left), one of the first office buildings completed during the 1980s downtown office-building orgy. Impressed with the relative good health of Inner Harbor real estate, Peter D. Leibowits Co. Inc., a Connecticut real estate developer, was considering turning 400 East Pratt into a 26-story office tower.

(Full size photographs follow)

LOOKING EAST FROM 400 BLOCK OF PRATT STREET, CIRCA 1915

Lombard and Gay Streets in 1940 was mostly a business-warehouse district of 1905–1915-era buildings like those at left which housed the Baltimore Nautical School and an odd assortment of packing, engineering and supply companies. Like Pratt Street a block south of it, center-city Lombard wasn't much to look at but it served its purpose in an era when much of what later became the Inner Harbor renewal area was ignored by persons other than those doing business there. Blocky and cold, the 1935 Bureau of Veterans Affairs building at right typified the architecture of Depression-era government buildings. *Peale Museum*

The early 1970s Inner Harbor Phase Two revitalization effort transformed Lombard Street into a gateway for Inner Harbor tourist attractions. One of them was the 1980 Holocaust Memorial, a portion of which is shown at left. A dozen years in the planning, it was the concept of Alvin D. Fisher who in 1968 thought it was time to educate the public about a terrible event, that since 1945 had been ignored by an indifferent press and buried by survivors too traumatized to discuss it. The city dedicated the ground and the Associated Jewish Charities raised the $360,000 to build it. Partly visible are the six rows of Bradford pear trees that symbolized the six million Jewish victims. The design, though, by Donald Kann & Associates and Arthur Valk (most of it not shown) proved an ideal roost for vagrants for whom nothing is sacred. About six weeks after the author took this early April view, the memorial was under demolition, including the six rows of Bradfords. Architect Jonathan Fishman designed a more "open" memorial, a $400,000 makeover dedicated 6 October 1997. The Community College of Baltimore's harbor campus, one block east, was conceived by CCB's longtime president Harry Bard to accommodate inner-city students; it opened in 1976.

This is what the southeast harbor business district looked like about a decade before the Great Fire flattened it. The view includes numerous 19th century city landmarks: Baltimore Exchange and Custom House (domed building at center), a Benjamin Latrobe and Maximilien Godefroy architectural collaboration built in 1819 and razed just two years before the fire (Lafayette was received here and Abraham Lincoln lay in state under the dome); Chamber of Commerce Building (1882), located just northwest of the Exchange; and the Sun Iron Building, southeast corner of Baltimore and South Streets (lower right corner); completed in 1851, it ushered in the age of iron front buildings in Baltimore. *Pratt*

This district needed almost total restoration after 1904. Remnants from that era include the Gayety Theatre (1906) at the southeast corner of Baltimore and Commerce Streets and the Chamber of Commerce (1906), in size and scale, similar to its 1882 predecessor. The 1991, 30-story Commerce Place (front) sat largely vacant before it became the Alex. Brown Building in 1997. The tower's near-full occupancy in early 1998 and its purchase in March (1998) by the New York-based Blackstone Group from Harlan/KDC (for about $80 million), underscored the remarkable comeback of downtown real estate. The roof at far left belongs to the 1980 Municipal Employees Credit Union Building, successor to the seedy Armistead Hotel at the southeast corner of E. Fayette and Holliday Streets. Note Candler Building, Power Plant, National Aquarium and Harbor View condo in the distance.

CAMDEN YARDS FROM BALTIMORE ARTS TOWER (ORIGINALLY EMERSON OR BROMO SELTZER TOWER), 1912

CAMDEN YARDS FROM BALTIMORE ARTS TOWER, APRIL 1996 *(Narrative follows)*

CAMDEN YARDS FROM BALTIMORE ARTS TOWER

YEAR 1912

INDUSTRY: Camden Yards was in its third metamorphosis here. The district of farms and estates of the late 18th century, where Comte Donatien de Rochambeau in 1781 bivouacked his troops en route to Yorktown, became in the early 19th century a residential hodgepodge of English and German immigrants, slaves and free blacks. Camden's residential character began to change in the mid-1850s with the arrival of the Baltimore and Ohio Railroad. Track construction, the $200,000 Niernsee and Nielson-designed Camden Station (1857–1866), shown with one of its original two side cupolas, and the B&O's 1898 warehouses (right, perpendicular to station) claimed blocks of residential space for commercial and industrial use. Note belching smokestacks of the Baltimore City Cold Storage Co. at Wayne and Eutaw Streets and the district's early 19th century residential units west of Eutaw (right) and south of Barre (two blocks south of Camden Street). The 1912 Polk City Directory lists one such residence/saloon—406 W. Conway Street—home of George Herman Ruth Sr., progenitor of an American icon to be. *B&O Railroad Museum*

APRIL 1996

SYNERGY: Urban renewal cleared most of the houses by the 1950s, leaving by the late 1970s one middle school and a few factories like the Parks Sausages plant. In 1979 Chessie Resources Inc. and a Washington-based developer proposed turning Camden Yards into another office tower/high-rent condo district. Then city and state officials, sobered by the Colts' sudden departure in March 1984 and the chance that Orioles owner Edward Bennett Williams might also take his business elsewhere, reconsidered. In April 1986 they created the Maryland Stadium Authority and came up with this: A multi-award winning gem of a ballpark (largely financed through proceeds from three sports lotteries, it opened April 1992) designed by Joe Spear of Kansas City-based HOK Sports Facilities Group, recycled 1898 warehouses quartering the Orioles' executive suites and a restored (to its post-Civil War configuration) Camden Station (March 1992). The ballpark's retro-chic design and close proximity to the Marc Line (note depot at rear of station) and I-95 lured fans from the Washington suburbs that had never set foot in the team's former home, Memorial Stadium. As of 1997, Camden Station was all form and no function, a pitiful waste of good space that private enterprise or some city agency might one day use, perhaps by fall 1998, when the Baltimore Ravens move into their own facility just south of Oriole Park. The 1980 Federal Reserve Building (left), another HOK design, stands at left, surrounded by a restored and rebuilt gentrified Otterbein neighborhood.

CIRCA 1914

1996

Located just east of Camden Yards, Inner Harbor West early in the century was a blue-collar, working class community of residential dwellings, churches, synagogues, businesses and manufactories producing everything from beer to chairs. Companies like Maryland Biscuit, American Biscuit, Globe Brewery, F.W. Felgner Tobacco and Heywood Brothers thrived here in Baltimore's smokestack era, when widget makers and cloth-cutters outnumbered numbers-crunchers and paper-pushers. Lombard Street is shown at lower left, veering westward off Liberty. The R.M. Sutton Company (foreground), a dry goods manufacturing firm established in 1890 from a restructuring of earlier partnerships, grew into the city's fourth largest concern of its kind. The block-long warehouses of the State and American Tobacco Companies (in background, just west of Light Street) dwarf contiguous industrial and residential harbor development. *Maryland Historical Society*

The only remnant of Inner Harbor West circa 1914 is the water itself, most of it blocked from view by the 24-story, 250 West Pratt Street office building. Completed in 1986, 250 West was designed by Skidmore, Owings and Merrill, the same firm responsible for Lever House of New York, a 1952 project that along with the Mies van der Rohe/Philip Johnson-designed Seagram Building, set the standard for all those post-war, lofty corporate blocks of glass and steel. The $150 million addition to the Baltimore Convention Center, shown under construction (right), added 185,000 square feet of exhibit space. A widened Lombard Street from foreground looking east shows the Days Inn (1984), the RTKL-designed Edward A. Garmatz Federal Courthouse (1976), NationsBank Center and the USF&G Tower. Note another RTKL design, Charles Center South (1975) at northwest corner of Charles and Lombard. The dark gray, glass-paneled building that critic Phoebe Stanton called a hinge between Charles Center and the newer Inner Harbor development, complements the district's two earlier office buildings of similar hue, One Charles Center and the Sun Life Insurance Building.

LOOKING SOUTHEAST FROM BALTIMORE ARTS TOWER

(Full size photographs follow)

LOOKING SOUTHEAST FROM BALTIMORE ARTS TOWER, CIRCA 1914

MODERN TIMES: Before Charles Center, there was the National Exchange Bank (triangular configured building in foreground), the B&O Building (1908, center), Jacob Epstein's Baltimore Bargain House (1903, with boomerang-shaped roofline, far left), the Fidelity Building (1897, left center), Tower Building (1912) and those other 1900-era office and commercial landmarks that formed Hopkins Place and the west-central business district just east of it. "The new buildings aspired to a solid and imposing style, and the new downtown had an ordered appearance, modern and comfortable, but overstuffed," wrote Sherry H. Olson in *Baltimore, The Building Of An American City. Maryland Historical Society*

MODERN, MODERN TIMES (NOT TO BE CONFUSED WITH POST-MODERN): By the mid 1950s, downtown didn't seem so new anymore. Vacant storefronts, a dearth of on-street parking and the suburban migration convinced a group of business leaders that revitalization was needed to keep downtown vibrant and competitive. In 1954 they formed the Committee for Downtown and raised $150,000 to commission a master plan. The powers that be were impressed: Mayor D'Alesandro and the City Council declared the district an urban renewal area; the Maryland Legislature voted to put the question of a $35,000,000 urban renewal loan on the November 1958 ballot. The people voted, the people approved, and thus Charles Center was born. It dismantled Hopkins Place and supplanted the Edwardian core of the west-central business district. The new buildings, no less solid and in size more imposing, redefined the post-war concept of what the downtown of a major American city was supposed to look like. Overstuffed it wasn't; overblown, perhaps. Shown is the jagged roof of the Civic Center (1962), to its right, the 1966–67 George H. Fallon Federal Building, "an IBM card with all the holes punched," quipped one critic. Shown proceeding left, the Morris Mechanic Theatre (1967), Mercantile Bank and Trust Building (1969) and Omni Hotel (1967). The roof (foreground) of the 14-story, 1993 City Crescent Building at 10 S. Howard Street contains an antenna farm manned by the Army Corps of Engineers for broadcasting purposes. An arm of the General Services Administration, the Corps leases over 50 percent of City Crescent's rental space.

(Narrative follows)

Monument Square Looking West, Circa 1890

Upscale residential district through the mid-19th century and always, as someone once wrote, a center for "commotions and alarms," Monument Square took its name—you guessed it— from the Godefroy-designed memorial honoring the veterans of Fort McHenry and Northpoint. Originally, a much taller monument to honor George Washington was planned here but citizens nixed the idea for fear the thing would topple over. Hence the less-lofty Battle Monument which took nearly 10 years (1815– 1825) to complete because of stormy seas that forced the ships importing the Italian marble to turn back. One resident of the Square, noted Baltimore attorney and U.S. Senator Reverdy Johnson, experienced first-hand in August 1835 the Square's riotous reputation. Following a bank crisis (Johnson was associated with the failed Bank of Maryland), rioters set fire to his stately mansion (far left, it was built in 1799 for wealthy merchant James A. Buchanan), destroying his furniture and $10,000 law library. Johnson rebuilt it and remained on the Square until Federal troops occupied it during the Civil War. Afterward, the city used the house for municipal offices, then razed it in 1893 for the widening of Fayette Street, just a year or so before two of the Square's other fixtures shown here, the circa 1830s St. Clair Hotel and the 1809 courthouse, came down to make room for the new courthouse. *Pratt*

Monument Square Looking West, 1993

The media still considers Monument Square, or Courthouse Square as it's been known in later years, a center for commotions and alarms. Local television stations often park their vehicles on the Monument's base to cover trials they deem newsworthy. Perhaps the most frenzied event of recent times occurred in January 1993, when convicted murderer Donte Carter leaped to freedom from a first-story courthouse window. Caught within 48 hours, Carter and his daring escape became part of court-house lore. Completed in December 1899 at a cost of $2,250,000, the Wyatte and Nolting-designed, Second Renaissance Revival-style courthouse (renamed in 1985 the Clarence Mitchell Court House in honor of the state senator and civil rights leader) will most likely be Baltimore's last on the site. In 1964, planners for Phase Two of Charles Center gave preservationists a good scare when they submitted a proposal to raze the courthouse. Nothing came of that madness or similar ideas circulating in the 1930s and 1940s to relocate the Battle Monument because of traffic congestion on Calvert Street. Preservationists in 1996 raised $250,000 to finance a face lift for the Monument. On 12 September 1997, as part of the city's bicentennial celebrations, it received a rousing dedication, replete with speeches and brass band.

Monument Square Looking East on Fayette Street, 1880s

Guy's Monument House originally occupied this 1820s-era building at the northeast corner of Calvert and Fayette Streets. It was a place "where gentlemen are treated as though they were in their own homes," wrote George W. Howard in his 1873 classic, *Monumental City.* Shown here in its last years, or possibly its last days, it was razed during this decade to make way for the United States Post Office. Guy's then moved across the street to the St. Clair. The Rennert House, seen just below the dome of City Hall, would soon be demolished as well and move elsewhere. *Pratt*

Monument Square Looking East on Fayette Street, 1994

This depression-era, block-sized post office building replaced a wild, high-Victorian, 1890 multi-towered thing that lasted only 40 years. The building shown here altered the once-diminutive scale of Monument Square east, giving it a mono-block appearance. The federal courthouse was also located here until the government in the 1970s built a new facility on Lombard Street, a move welcomed by a backlogged Baltimore City Circuit Court which expanded into what became known as Courthouse East.

Preston Gardens Looking North from Courthouse
1920, 1937, 1994

The auto age sort of snuck up on the horse-and-buggy age, then pounced, prompting cities to launch massive urban renewal projects like Preston Gardens. Dedicated in 1919, the place a year later showed fresh cement and newly-planted saplings that would grow to shade generations of downtown office workers on break or taking their lunch. The city still hadn't figured out what to do with all the cars, pictured here parked every which way, parallel, perpendicular, diagonally. Numerous 19th century residential dwellings still lined the west side of St. Paul Street, reminders of when the area had been home to the Warfields, Swans, Gilmors, Dulanys and other prominent families, most of whom had left by the early teens. The houses would soon fall for commercial interests.

Domed roof of the old 1884 Baltimore Polytechnic Institute (Poly moved to North Avenue in 1911) is shown on the east side of St. Paul Street. In a 1928 essay, Gerald W. Johnson, the great Baltimore journalist, defended Preston Gardens against critics who thought it should have been turned into one massive parking garage: "A great slash cut through the business district and producing nothing more profitable than grass and flowers seems an eccentricity; and to the thoroughly standardized American eccentricity is the unpardonable sin. . . . It (Preston Gardens) is an offense to the popular idols of standardization and conformity. It is not dull, therefore it is an offense in the eyes of dull men, who are unfortunately numerous."

Two-way traffic, still the norm on St. Paul Street and other major arteries in 1937, created daily cases of gridlock that would not be relieved until the advent of one-way streets in the 1940s. The recently-completed Orleans Street viaduct (west ramp shown in center of photo) improved the flow of crosstown traffic. The 15-story, 1922 Stanbalt Building (501 St. Paul Place), once offices for the Standard Oil Corporation, and new office buildings along St. Paul's west side emphasize how commercial this district had become in 17 years. The early 1930s office building on the northwest corner of St. Paul and Saratoga Streets housed all manner of tenants, including Rose Exterminators, Eck's Tailors, St. Paul Finance, the Southern Insurance Agency and attorney Ruth S. Newman.

Preston Gardens, three-quarters of a century after its completion, still worked as an attractive, intelligent solution to accommodating downtown traffic. The "great slash cut through the business district producing nothing more profitable than grass and flowers" (but for some reason there are fewer tulip beds than there used to be) has had few alterations, notwithstanding the massive office buildings that sprang up around it like the 1957 Fidelity and Deposit Company of Maryland (northwest corner of Saratoga and St. Paul Streets), its next door neighbor, C&P Telephone (1940) and Mercy Hospital (1963), located where the old Poly once stood. It's still a decent place for an urban picnic and provides reserved parking for Circuit Court judges (left) and police personnel (right). Nostalgia for the intimate, old Courtland Street district died through the decades along with Baltimoreans born early enough to remember it.

PRESTON GARDENS LOOKING NORTH FROM COURTHOUSE, 1920, *PEALE MUSEUM*

COURTLAND STREET LOOKING NORTH FROM LEXINGTON STREET, 1914

Here's a rare glimpse of Courtland Street two years before demolition crews razed the west side (left) of it for Preston Gardens. Trees shade a narrow street in the days when automobiles could park just about anywhere toll free. Four blocks long, Courtland ran between St. Paul and Calvert Streets through the heart of the city's legal district. *Pratt*

ST. PAUL PLACE LOOKING NORTH FROM LEXINGTON STREET, 1994

Eight decades later, the city's legal machinery still kept the courthouse district humming with activity during business days. Pre-World War One era building at right housed the Office of the Public Defender into the late 1990s.

In scale and proportion, Belgian-blocked, pre-Preston Gardens St. Paul Street between Franklin and Centre Streets blended right into tiny Hamilton Street (left), a choice address for social clubs and attorneys who had an easy walking commute to their offices. Some readers might recognize the 1850s-era Italianate rowhouses on St. Paul's east side north of Centre Street. They survived Preston Gardens only to be razed in the late 1960s for an apartment complex. *Sun File Photo*

After Preston Gardens, Hamilton Street, with its narrow, hip-roofed carriage houses, appeared as a quaint remnant from another age, isolated from a widened, "automobile-ready" St. Paul Street. While lacking the near-perfect fit of its predecessor, the teens-era office building at northwest corner of Hamilton and St. Paul looks like it belongs here. Offices just north of it are the only 19th century buildings in this view that survived. The row on St. Paul's east side in earlier view gave way to the Waterloo Place apartments.

The Porter Building (southwest corner of St. Paul Place and Saratoga Street), a four-story, early 19th century rowhouse built in the Federal style, typified the kind of house designed for wealthy Baltimoreans of the period. Later renovated into attorneys' offices, it stood vacant as of 1929, awaiting demolition. The Florentine-style, Maryland Historical Society (1848–1918), another area landmark that stood at the northwest corner, came down around the same time. *Pratt*

The 33-story, 222 St. Paul Place was built in 1965 as an apartment/office complex. In 1984, as tourism was gaining momentum as an industry in Baltimore, it became the Tremont Plaza Hotel. St. Paul Plaza, an office complex just south of it, arrived in 1989. A remnant from the Federalist period and since 1908 offices for the Warfield-founded *Daily Record* newspaper, is shown just west of the Tremont.

ST. PAUL STREET LOOKING SOUTH FROM CENTRE STREET, 1936

St. Paul Street Looking South from Centre Street, 1936

Cars, cars, everywhere! Motorists back in 1936 had to contend with two-way major arteries and poorly synchronized traffic signals. And just think: The JFX was still 26 years away. The view includes the historic "chimney corner" house (southwest corner of St. Paul and Centre Streets), said to date from the year 1812, a time when much of the city north of Saratoga Street lay bare and unsettled. Originally a residence, it housed a number of businesses that came and went like the busy crosstown traffic passing by its doorstep through the decades. There are still Baltimoreans who can recall when it served as a tea room in the 1920s. But its most famous resident was probably Enrico Liberti, a nationally-known cabinet maker skilled enough to earn commissions from the Kennedy White House and State of Maryland (he built 14 New York-style Sheraton chairs for the White House and 37 pieces of Hepplewhite-style desks and armchairs for the Maryland State House senate chamber). Liberti practiced his craft here from 1930 until his retirement in 1977. *Pratt*

St. Paul Street Looking South from Centre Street, 1994

St. Paul Street became one-way (north) in the late 1940s, but it was really internationally renowned traffic engineer Henry A. Barnes who deserves credit for unclogging the city's arteries, slowing the advanced case of arteriosclerosis that had been advancing since the debut of the Ford Model T. Soon after Barnes arrived in June 1953, he reversed the one-way traffic flow on St. Paul Street and other streets, outlawed left turns at certain intersections and modernized the signal system. "Expressways are fine," he once said, "but until they're built, we've got to make the best use of the streets we have." Barnes did, then left Baltimore for New York in January 1962, several months before completion of the JFX. Through interviews, the author learned of a possible Barnes connection to the chimney corner house. Concerned about the odd way the house juts out toward the intersection, Barnes allegedly wanted it torn down to make it easier for motorists turning right onto St. Paul from Centre. A petition drive saved the house, the story goes, and the only concession to motorists was the removal of some sidewalk. Struever Brothers, Eccles and Rouse renovated it in 1985 for the law offices of R. Roland Brockmeyer. Future traffic czars take note: The house is protected by the National Register of Historic Places.

Light Street Looking North from Pratt Street, 1911

C.C. Giese, J.G. Leake, Palmer-Harvey, A. Reiter, Frey & Son, Carborundum, Prager & Miller, Sabaco Pump, Schoenewolf . . . The eclectic mix of printers, grocers and supply companies housed in these post-1904 era S. Light Street office buildings (124–128, left; 121–123, right) are as forgotten as the buildings themselves. The marbled circa 1906 National Bank of Baltimore building at northeast corner of Light and Baltimore Streets was razed in the mid-1970s. *Pratt*

Light Street Looking North from Pratt Street, 1994

Light Street for the past 25 years has been associated with names like Signet Bank, Maryland National Bank, NationsBank, Fairfax (later Susquehanna) and USF&G. One building that survived from 1911 is 31 Light Street on the northeast corner of Pratt and Lombard (at right, just north of parking garage). The photo shows it in its 1970s, Mies van der Rohe modernism guise, all dressed up in tacky metal cladding with nowhere to go except back to the future. Sure enough, Gould Architects and Wilhelm Builders in September 1996 completed their "re-restoration" (exposing the original masonry) of 31 Light Street for the building's owners, Miller Corporate Real Estate.

The old Southern Hotel (right, just below Signet Tower) was another offspring of the Great Fire, which destroyed the Carrollton, its predecessor. It opened in 1918, closed in 1964. As of March 1998 it sat sealed and empty. J.J. Clarke developers aimed to build a 34-story office/hotel/restaurant/parking complex on the site. The proposed 1 Light Street Tower would contain about 300,000 square feet of class A office space—an intrepid project indeed, considering the fortunes other developers lost a few years earlier from over-building in a recessed market.

(Full size photographs follow)

LIGHT STREET LOOKING NORTH FROM PRATT STREET, 1911

1912

1936

1994

100 Block of E. Baltimore Street
Looking West Toward Light Street
1912, 1936, 1994

A Hughes Company photographer took this spirited, pre-World War One scene on the "new" Baltimore Street. The Great Fire was still fresh in the collective memory of Baltimoreans justly proud of their speedy recovery and modern downtown, a portion of which is seen here. The circa 1905–1907 commercial structures, including the National Bank of Baltimore (northeast corner), pale beside the 1908 B&O Building at Charles and Baltimore Streets.

Twenty-four years later, the same buildings sport new storefronts and protruding electric signs, and asphalt blankets the street's former cobbled surface. Gone are the last vestiges of the horse-and-buggy age, as trolleys now compete with automobiles for street space. Baltimoreans in 1936 were hardly ready to end the New Deal: On May 4th they voted for FDR over anti-New Dealer Henry Breckinridge by a margin of six to one. The "new" north side of E. Baltimore Street lasted 70 years, then tumbled in the mid-1970s for subway construction and corporate high-rise development, forcing Needle's Liquors, Western Union and Century Shoe Repair (shown) to relocate. Waldorph Tuxedo, Household Finance, Thomas and Thompson Drugs, Gordon's Booksellers and Card Mart, fronting on the block's north side as late as 1973, moved elsewhere before the wrecking ball struck. Half the block just west of Light Street came down (for 6 St. Paul Street) in the early 1980s, ending the tenure of longtime retail concerns like Robert Reed Hats, Stutman's Men's Wear and Regal Shoes. Among the casualties was Cy Bloom's Brass Rail at 22 E. Baltimore Street, a favorite bar and eatery of local celebrities and politicians. The block's south side remained largely intact through the 1990s, including Fader's (in 1912 it sold its cigars one block east and across the street).

The three post-modern corporate titans shown in the recent view—the RTKL-designed Crestar Bank Building (1989, 120 E. Baltimore Street, formerly Bank of Baltimore), Signet Bank (1985, 7 St. Paul Street) and Citibank (1985, 6 St. Paul Street)—epitomize the post-war age of bigness, where one building takes up space once shared by three. Critics of modern corporate architecture often cite the cold, alienating quality of elevated "bottom-level" offices and tinted, permanently-shut windows that keep the outside world from looking in. Writer-pontificator Norman Mailer, who usually has something to say about everything, feels one-way windows are a prime example of "violence by the state" (as opposed to "violence by the individual"). Note facade of the 16-story W. R. Grace Building shown just west of 6 St. Paul Street. It was designed by the Philadelphia-based firm of Bower and Fradley and completed in early 1972. Critic Phoebe B. Stanton thought it added a classic richness to downtown without garish excess: "It is handsome, but it is not stylistically aggressive. It is elegant although it has none of the fashionable mannerisms and flourishes that can date a building . . ." Sheathed in brown-hued brick and designed with street-level retail space (occupied at various times by The Dark Room, Hanover Shoes, Hess Shoes, Gordon's Booksellers), the building exudes a warmer presence than its three glassbound, stilted neighbors to the east.

SOUTHEAST CORNER OF BALTIMORE AND CALVERT STREETS, 1906

ON THE MEND: Evidence of Baltimore's speedy recovery from the 1904 fire can be seen here. In two years, Calvert between Baltimore Street and the harbor was nearly whole again, thanks in part to $29 million paid out in insurance claims and $5 million in start-up money the city obtained in 1903 from Mayor Hayes's (the fire postponed the mayor's plans to install a new sewer system) sale of Western Maryland Railroad stock. The imposing 1901 Continental Trust Building, literally a shell of its former self after the fire, looks almost totally restored. Designed by D.H. Burnham and Company, it was a direct architectural offspring of the Commercial or Chicago-style created through the work of William Le Baron Jenny, Louis Sullivan and others. Daniel H. Burnham inspected the damage personally, then assured the building's owners that the steel frame was structurally-sound enough to rebuild on. Under construction just south of Continental Trust is the Keyser Building, southeast corner of Calvert and Redwood Streets. *Library of Congress*

SOUTHEAST CORNER OF BALTIMORE AND CALVERT STREETS, 1996

One Calvert Plaza, formerly Continental Trust, was in better shape than many grade B downtown office buildings in the late 1990s. Used as offices for attorneys and various city agencies, it was 72 percent occupied and under study by its owner, Principal Mutual Life Insurance Company, for an exterior renovation. Note how the scale and proportion of S. Calvert Street below Baltimore Street has remained relatively intact since the fire. Shown in this and the earlier view is the Wyatt and Sperry-designed 1886 Old Mercantile Safe Deposit and Trust Company Building, northeast corner of Calvert and Redwood Streets. The exterior of this Romanesque-style architectural powerhouse fared much better in the fire than its neighbors, receiving little structural damage to its thick brick walls; the interior burned after debris from the Continental Building crashed through the Old Mercantile's skylight. The author shot this view *through* a 7th floor garage window in the Crestar Bank Building. Fixed windows are the downside of climate-controlled, modern office buildings for photographers needing unobstructed, panoramic views.

Baltimore and Liberty Streets, the north end of Hopkins Place, was a frenzy of wholesale activity just prior to World War One. Jacob Epstein, a Jewish-Lithuanian immigrant who made millions in the wholesale clothing business, built the circa 1903 building (it just escaped being consumed in the 1904 fire) at right for his Baltimore Bargain House, an empire that also included warehouses and retail outlets at 213–221 W. Fayette, Scott and Wicomico Streets and 10–12 N. Howard Street. The statue at left, erected there in 1911, is a memorial to John Mifflin Hood, president of the Western Maryland Railroad between 1874–1902. *Maryland Historical Society*

Urban renewal in the 1960s destroyed just about every landmark along Hopkins Place except the old Epstein building, which continues to give the northwest corner of Liberty and Baltimore Streets its familiar grand sweep. Gage Men's Wear, a retail institution established in the late 1940s, moved into the first floor in 1966. Critics who claim the 1962 Baltimore Arena (left) was obsolete before the paint dried tend to overlook its utilitarianism: The building has staged everything from the Barnum and Bailey Circus to professional (when Baltimore had the Bullets) and college basketball games, ice hockey and soccer, to rock and roll concerts. Plans to tear it down have been in the offing for years. The 1993 City Crescent Building (10 S. Howard Street) just behind it added some sparkle to the drab, run-down S. Howard Street area. Designed by the Washington, D.C.-based Weihe Design Group, it was 98 percent occupied as of late 1997, housing a NationsBank branch and government agencies. Otis Warren, a partner, credits Light Rail, among other reasons, for its success. Mr. Hood, meanwhile, was moved in 1962 to Preston Gardens where he faces Mercy Hospital. In Baltimore, old monuments never die, they just get relocated.

A southbound view of Hopkins Place shows the 1907 columned National Exchange Bank (right, center) and the Salvage Corps Building with its fire crew posing at left. Note Jacob Epstein's American Wholesale Corporation at far right (Baltimore and Liberty Streets); in 1930 Epstein and his partners had sold the business to the Chicago-based Butler Brothers. Developed between 1875–1920, "Hopkins Place," wrote Carleton Jones in *Lost Baltimore Landmarks*, "had a certain sweep to it, a cosmopolitanism that reminded one of the crosstown squares of Manhattan as Broadway does its great diagonal through that city. It was a similar, wholly urban environment in the best sense, lively and the hub of city wholesaling." *Peale Museum*

Late 1950s renewal for Charles Center unraveled the great bow tie street pattern that made Hopkins Place so unique. Landmarks shown include the Omni International Hotel (1967), the 24-story, Peterson and Brickbauer and Emory Roth and Sons-designed Mercantile Safe Deposit and Trust Company (1969) and Baltimore Arena. If the city's latest plans to raze the Arena go through, this so-called sprawling mass of obsolescence would be the second building of the early Charles Center era to come down. The old Hamburger's, which spanned Fayette Street at Charles for so long (since 1963) that many Baltimoreans cannot remember when it didn't, became the first; its owner, Peter G. Angelos, had part of it dismantled in early 1998. 250 W. Pratt Street is shown nestled against the southwestern horizon in all its grand ubiquity.

LIBERTY STREET LOOKING SOUTH FROM FAYETTE STREET, 1994

Robert Rennert invested the $275,000 the government had paid him for his hotel on Monument Square to build Baltimore's third (and last) Rennert. It opened in October 1885 and soon became famous for oysters, terrapins (both were shipped north to impress New York gourmets) and political deal-making. The Rennert was at its peak in 1918, still basking in the afterglow of the 1912 Democratic convention, when its elegant dining room was filled with delegates meeting at the Fifth Regiment Armory. The Rennert had a political as well as a geographic connection to St. Paul's Rectory (center) in those days. Reverend Dr. Arthur B. Kinsolving, rector of St. Paul's (from 1906 through the 1940s), protested a city engineer's plan to cut back the Saratoga Street terrace by several feet, and voiced his displeasure to then Democratic boss "Sonny" Mahon who held court in the Rennert's lobby. Moved by Kinsolving's case, Mahon, who was Catholic, took it before the Board of Estimates and killed the engineer's proposal with this: "This damned thing has got to stop. Dr. Kinsolving is my pastor!" *Maryland Historical Society*

The Rennert never recovered from its financial difficulties after the onset of prohibition in 1919. It closed in 1939 and was razed in 1941. The 450-space Rennert Garage, an outrageous moniker considering the elegance it replaced, occupied the site from 1950 until owner Mullan Enterprises razed it in 1996 for a 56-space surface lot. St. Paul's Rectory, its design an architectural hybrid of "late Georgian-early Republican expression," to quote *Maryland Historical Magazine*, is protected by the National Register of Historic Places. Built in 1791, it outlived the Rennert and most likely will see the towers of Two Charles Center tumble for something else.

LIBERTY STREET LOOKING NORTH FROM LEXINGTON STREET, 1994

The 1904 fire spared what was then Baltimore's garment district, where men, women and children, many of them Jewish immigrants from Eastern Europe, labored on the lofts of the city's hulking warehouses. Shown here is the 300 block of W. Baltimore Street, once (along with the 400 block) a veritable showcase of cast-iron storefronts. Used most extensively from the 1840s to about 1900, cast iron was a favorite of builders who appreciated its fire-resistant quality—no consolation to the dozens of cast iron storefront businesses destroyed in the fire. In 1906 the six-story, iron-front Abell Building (right), built in 1878 by *Sun* mogul A.S. Abell as an investment, housed Phoenix Cigar and the Isaac Friedenwald Company, "the largest and best-equipped printers, lithographers and engravers in the South," according to an 1898 edition of *Frank Leslie's Illustrated Newspaper. Pratt*

By the late 1990s, Baltimore had but ten iron-front buildings left, six in the 300 and 400 blocks of W. Baltimore Street alone. The Abell, listed on the National Register of Historic Places, became a symbol of the district's demise as a once thriving manufacturing center. As late as the early 1970s, the building was close to full occupancy. Nine tenants were left by 1990, only about three as of 1997. The building's present owners harbor sanguine visions of a renovated, fully occupied Abell supported by the ever-expanding University of Maryland complex hungry for more commercial and/or residential space. When is the question: "It could happen in 1998 or 2005," the landlord told the author. A revival of the long comatose Hippodrome Theater (12 N. Eutaw Street) might also help revive the ailing Abell and stimulate business for area retail concerns like Sunny's Surplus (left), a landmark since 1963.

DEATH . . . Time was running out for Baltimore and Hanover as Baltimoreans had known it. Construction crews were already busy turning the unit block of West Lexington Street into what became Charles Center North. A portion of Charles Center South, completed by the late 1960s, would be located here. As late as 1960, S. Hanover Street between Baltimore and Pratt Streets claimed a dozen clothing stores, seven shoe stores, three jewelry shops and sundry other businesses including Safeway Fur Service, Loeb Dykeman Co., Overbrook Egg Nog and the Maryland Notion House. Many had vacated by 1962. Bond Clothiers had been a retail fixture at 27 West Baltimore Street since at least 1938. The old Sun Building had graced the southwest corner of Baltimore and Charles Streets since 1906. Both came down for construction of the Morris A. Mechanic Theatre. *Courtesy of M.E. Warren*

. . . AND TRANSFIGURATION . . . The unit block of S. Hanover Street gave way in the late 1960s to Hopkins Plaza, centerpiece of Charles Center South, which included the George H. Fallon Federal Building (1967), Morris A. Mechanic Theatre and the Mercantile Safe Deposit and Trust Building (1969). The Mechanic opened 16 January 1967 with "Hello Dolly" (Betty Grable appeared in the starring role), six months after its chief benefactor and namesake died of a heart attack. Designed by John M. Johansen of Seattle, the intimate theatre was built with a seating capacity of 1,600. *Architectural Forum* named it and One Charles Center "among the outstanding U.S. architectural works of the 1960s." Uncertainty has dogged the Mechanic on and off since the mid-1970s. Perhaps the most serious threat to its existence came in early 1998 with the proposed renovation of the long-vacant 1914 Hippodrome Theatre. With a potential seating capacity of 2,300, the old Hipp could stage large-scale musicals ("The Phantom of the Opera," "Miss Saigon," "Beauty and the Beast") that bypass Baltimore for lack of space. The Mechanic's current lease runs to the year 2000. After that, who knows? Hopkins Plaza's $4 million renovation that began in November 1997 with the removal of pedestrian skywalks spared the one shown spanning Baltimore Street. A classic Greek temple design (Parker and Thomas) like the 1907 First Union National Bank (originally the Savings Bank of Baltimore) building, shown just east of the metro stop, never looks out of place or vogue, no matter what is built around it.

UNIT BLOCK OF W. LEXINGTON STREET LOOKING WEST, CIRCA 1925

PRIME TIME: Forty years before Charles Center, the unit block of W. Lexington Street cut through to Liberty and claimed over a dozen stores. Intimate and bustling with automobile and pedestrian traffic, the street holds exciting memories for those old enough to recall when Kay Jewelry, Queen Quality Boot Shop, Huyler's Confectionary, Wyman's Shoes, Goldenburg's, Dann's, Altmann Millinery, Hahn Shoes, Bachrach's Photo Studio and O'Neills' Department Store (southwest corner of Charles and Lexington) thrived here. In 1925 the street featured two relatively new movie houses, the Valencia and Century, in the year movie-goers took in late-silent era hits like "The Phantom of The Opera" (Lon Chaney), "The Gold Rush" (Charlie Chaplin) and "Stella Dallas" (Belle Bennett). At Hahn's, "good-looking black and tan Oxfords" could be had for $12; at Bachrach's, $10 bought a dozen portrait photos; and for those with money to burn, upscale O'Neills' sold their top-of-the-line Costume Suit, "the smartest of all smart fashions," for $350. Originally part of the Whitehurst chain, the Valencia and Century closed a few years after 1955, the year Morris A. Mechanic purchased them from Whitehurst. O'Neills' opened in 1882, survived the 1904 fire by a wind gust and served a loyal clientele until it closed in 1954, seven years before the building came down for One Charles Center. The granite-walled Fidelity Building (right) would be the street's only structural anchor to the pre-Charles Center era after 1961, the year construction crews began breaking ground. *Peale Museum*

UNIT BLOCK OF W. LEXINGTON STREET LOOKING WEST, 1995

LESS IS MORE? The unit block of W. Lexington Street vanished under Charles Center Plaza. Office workers once patronized this place in droves before Harborplace lured them away and the Plaza became the preserve of vagrants and panhandlers. It also lost favor with some preservationists and post-modern urban designers less than enamored with barren, wind-swept plazas, glass-walled office towers, underground parking garages and pedestrian ramps, the very features some post-war urban planners found so appealing. Acting on a late 1980s New York-based urban design consultant's recommendation to bring cars and people back on one level, the Schmoke administration removed Center Plaza's pedestrian walkways several years before the skyramps surrounding Hopkins Plaza came down. City Hall opposed Peter G. Angelos' early 1998 proposal to bury Center Plaza under a 200-space surface lot. The vagrants and panhandlers, we can surmise, didn't like it much either.

Charles Center Plaza was a work in progress in 1964. The Mies van der Rohe-designed One Charles Center office building (left) stands amid its aging predecessors (B&O Building, BG&E Building) and ongoing construction. Completed in 1962 in only 13 months, it was the first building to arrive on the 33 acre site and housed (in 1964) an eclectic mix of government and quasi-government agencies (Baltimore Neighborhoods, Inc., Metropolitan Transit Authority), insurance companies (Crown Life), lawyers' offices (Milton B. Allen) and financial institutions (T. Rowe Price). Casual Corner, a trendy clothing store for women, located here early on and stayed into 1998. Pounded into rubble and barely discernable as a street, the first block of West Lexington became a conduit for downtown office workers. Fueled by $40 million in public expenditures and another $145 million in private investment, Charles Center was more than 80 percent completed by the late 1960s. *courtesy of M.E. Warren*

The Two Charles Center (left) apartments (1969), the American National Bank building (1985) and the Fisher, Nes, Campbell-designed 1966 addition to the BG&E Company surround what became Center Plaza. By the late 1990s, Charles Center sat infirm and ailing, surrounded by several economic development groups (Charles Street Association, Greater Baltimore Committee, Downtown Partnership of Baltimore, Inc. and a coalition led by Orioles owner Peter G. Angelos and David W. Kornblatt) voicing their ideas for its revitalization. Angelos owned the old Hamburger's building (vacant as of late 1997) and One Charles Center, Kornblatt the 28-story St. Paul Plaza office tower. The situation thus made for a delicate balance between personal and public interests, a balance that existed from the very beginning and that some felt favored the former. Wrote David Harvey in *The Baltimore Book, New Views Of Local History*: "Charles Center was conceived and built as a property development scheme of direct benefit to corporate and finance capital. The city as a whole received very little benefit from it."

Charles Street Looking North from Saratoga Street
1878, 1937, 1995

Industry, commerce, noise and crowds pushed the city's monied class from the harbor in a straight northbound direction along what became the Charles Street corridor, Baltimore's Main Line if there ever was one. From the late Federal, early Greek Revival period (1820–1850) through much of the 19th century, Charles Street from Saratoga to the Washington Monument was both exclusive and exclusively residential. Much of the block shown here went up in the 1830s and 1840s, way before it became known as a snooty, upscale shopping district. Back then, it was just a snooty, upscale residential district, home to families that could afford to retreat to sprawling country estates during the summer months. Some of the salient design features of antebellum town homes built for the wealthy can be seen here, most notably the three-story design; as late as 1840 only 10 percent of the city's new homes had three stories. The two-story houses at lower right might date from the 1790s, a time when Charles Street beyond Saratoga was little more than a footpath meandering northward through swampy countryside.

The commercial invasion began around 1880 and accelerated after the 1904 fire. The fire consumed Charles Street below Lexington, necessitating the need for more retail space. Commercialism redesigned, in some cases, discarded altogether the block's Federal-style architectural wardrobe. Medical and law offices, clothing stores, tailor shops, jewelers, gift shops, etc. proliferated. The 11-story, art deco, Mottu and White-designed Baltimore Life Building (at right, with arched entrance way) supplanted four houses in the earlier view, though period maps indicate there were post-1878 buildings that preceded it. Built 1929–1930, it quartered, among the many doctors' and lawyers' offices in 1937, the Berlitz School of Languages. Moving north toward Franklin Street, we see the surviving Federal-style homes draped in their 20th century, commercial attire: swell-front facades, bay windows and in the case of one house (fifth from Baltimore Life Building), a fourth floor. The double-decker bus, shown passing Pleasant Street, was part of the United Railways' A Line. Double-deckers ran up Charles Street from the early 1920s to 1942.

The C&P Telephone Building (1971), shown at right in the recent view, erased more of the block's Federalist past, wiping out four of the original houses and irking area merchants in the process. In a 1973 *Sun* article, merchants railed against the building, claiming it was out of proportion to the street, destroyed potential retail space and aggravated the already poor parking situation. In late 1992 the city gave merchants and their customers a big break, allowing 24-hour metered parking. Kinko's Copiers (left), occupying the multi-renovated, Niernsee and Neilson-designed former 1873 YMCA Building, was one such beneficiary.

**CHARLES STREET
LOOKING NORTH
FROM
SARATOGA STREET,**
1878, *PRATT*

CHARLES STREET LOOKING NORTH FROM SARATOGA STREET, 1937, *PRATT*

This steep grade of a street, once a popular course with winter sledders who lived nearby, is a remnant from the great cliffs that in the 18th century sloped eastward toward the Jones Falls stream valley. By the late 19th century, long after the cliffs had been graded, Calvert and Franklin was a busy place. The Niernsee and Neilson-designed, Italiante Calvert Station was here, its entrance angled in a peculiar southwesterly direction. The Grand Central (left) and Windsor (right) hotels added to the heavy traffic. Built in 1850 for the Baltimore and Susquehanna Railroad (subsequently the Northern Central R.R. and Pennsylvania R.R.), the station served as a makeshift hospital during the Battle of Gettysburg. The Grand Central and Windsor were popular with out-of-towners seeking convenient, moderately priced lodging. Note how Franklin Street extended all the way to Guilford Avenue (then North Street), then the site of various manufactories producing everything from grave stones and whiskey to lumber and leather. *Pratt*

Some didn't like it, including the grumpy, old H.L. Mencken, but management at the Baltimore *Sun* in the late 1940s decided to relocate (the old 1906 Sun Building at Baltimore and Charles Streets survived until 1964) at the site of the long-abandoned Calvert Station. Opened in late 1950, the new Sun Building cut off Franklin Street between Calvert Street and Guilford Avenue per the design specifications of Palmer, Fisher, Williams & Nes, the architectural firm hired by the Abell Co. Shown is the $16 million addition, completed in 1981 to house new presses and other equipment. The 1973 Shillman Building (500 N. Calvert Street) stands on site of the old Grand Central. Shillcraft, Inc. occupied it from the time it was built until the company moved to Essex in 1986. In August 1993 the State of Maryland, continuing its early 1990s shopping spree of downtown office buildings, approved the building's purchase for $3.5 million from Haron Dahan, a Harford County homebuilder.

H. C. KLOTS
WHOLESALE TO THE
PLUMBING & HEATING

MONUMENT AND CALVERT STREETS, 1936

(Narrative follows)

MONUMENT AND CALVERT STREETS

1936

This is Waterloo Row, architect Robert Mills' famed 1815–1819 masterpiece of urban housing built out in what was then considered the boonies. Initially the row was a financial flop, ironically for the same reason its investors thought it would sell: location, location, location. The row's distance from the city's center, coupled with the fact that it faced a swamp, dissuaded buyers who balked at traveling that far just for the privilege of living near the soon-to-be-completed Washington Monument (another Mills design) and manor lord John Eager Howard, who lived near the present intersection of Chase and Calvert Streets. The development's initial rejection by the elite social class for whom Mills designed it proved a windfall for the craftsmen who built it, as they became its first generation of residents. Multiple renovations, extensive street work and just plain neglect turned these poor houses into something Mills would barely recognize. Plans were on the drawing board, literally, in 1936 to restore the

12 houses, but nothing came of them. The city razed Waterloo Row in 1970 (for a Boise-Cascade Corporation luxury apartment complex that fell through), and subsequently the ire of some preservationists who never forgave. *Pratt*

1994

This is Waterloo Place, developed by Summit Properties between 1989–1991 for an upscale, urbane clientele desiring in-town luxury apartment living. David Furman, whose architectural firm designed it, informed the author that he based the design on Mt. Vernon's existing structures, not on the venerated row. One of Summit's executives "played" Robert Mills at the grand opening, pulling up in horse and carriage attired in period clothing. Like the developers of Waterloo Row, Summit used its property's proximity to the Washington Monument and Mount Vernon Place as a selling point, one that apparently caught on. As of late 1997 the occupancy rate stood at 98 percent; rents ranged from $815–$1,610.

CIRCA 1910

1994

Waterloo Row's investors meant to capitalize on the site of the Washington Monument and Belvedere, John Eager Howard's estate. Howard's heirs had the same idea, only they were a lot more successful. After Howard's death in 1827, they subdivided (Mount Vernon was Baltimore's first subdivision) what was then called "Howard's Woods" and quickly sold lots to well-heeled Baltimoreans. One, Edward McDonald Greenway, Sr., built in 1835 the first house on what later became West Mount Vernon Place. The view shows the square as it looked around 1910, shortly before its relandscaping and six years after the powerful Municipal Arts Society, most of whom were Mount Vernon residents, had successfully petitioned Maryland Governor Warfield to sign the "Anti-Skyscraper Bill," prohibiting the erection of buildings (churches excepted) more than 70 feet high within one block of the Monument. It was the "huge" and "ungainly" (as a *Sun* critic described it in 1907) 10-story Severn Flats apartments (shown at right), built in 1895, that had triggered the Society's outrage. Theodore Marburg, the Society's president, lived two doors east of the Severn at 14 West. The domed structure, two or three blocks distant, is the old Johns Hopkins observatory. *Pratt*

(Full size photographs follow)

Mount Vernon remained the turf of Baltimore Society well into the 20th century. Still, even as early as 1924, the migration outward had already begun: "It is no idle jest that Baltimore Society is moving farther and farther out and from all signs soon there will be no more Baltimore Society, literally speaking, as everyone will live in the country," wrote a Johns Hopkins student in the *Sun*. 1924 was the year the newly formed Baltimore Museum of Art established temporary quarters in the Mary Garrett house on the southwest corner of Cathedral and Monument Streets, shown in the 1910 view. After the museum vacated the house for its Wyman Park facility in 1929, residents met to discuss a proposed 12 story apartment building on the site, one block away from the restricted district, but close enough to cause discomfort. One resident lamented that since the place had "degenerated into a runaway for dogs and a gathering place for night hawks," apartment buildings would be preferable to cheap rooming houses. The Mount Vernon Apartments, built shortly thereafter, became the luxurious Peabody Court Hotel in 1985, the equally luxurious Latham Hotel in 1992 and the not-as-luxurious Clarion in 1995. Clarion did away with room service and fine dining, a move that maximized the bottom line but minimized the number of showbiz celebs that had patronized the Peabody Court and Latham. Peabody Conservatory students, like the one seen here toting her instrument, probably outnumber Mt. Vernon's dogs and night hawks.

WEST MOUNT VERNON PLACE

WEST MOUNT VERNON PLACE, CIRCA 1910

WASHINGTON PLACE LOOKING NORTH FROM CENTRE STREET, 1914

The view looks north from Charles and Centre Streets during the last days of the "good old days," when horses still mingled with automobiles, ragtime was in the air and 60 percent of Baltimore Society still lived in Bolton Hill and Mount Vernon. *University of Maryland Baltimore County*

WASHINGTON PLACE LOOKING NORTH FROM CENTRE STREET, 1994

Mount Vernon landmarks like the 1849, Niernsee and Neilson-designed Francis Jencks house (left) and the 1862–1878 Peabody Conservatory (right) will probably survive well into the 21st century. During the fight to keep high-rises and commercialism out, Municipal Arts Society member Dr. Henry Barton Jacobs said this: "The present residents of these squares will pass away. Their interest will cease, but the squares if preserved, and the Monument, will live on through countless generations, still the pride of all Baltimoreans." That might also include the Flower Mart, a Baltimore/Mount Vernon tradition dating from 1911. Threatened with extinction in the mid-1990s, the Women's Civic League-sponsored May rite of spring rebounded in 1997.

CHARLES STREET LOOKING NORTH TOWARD FRANKLIN STREET, 1910

QUIESCENCE: A street cleaner goes about his work on a Charles Street free of automobile traffic and, for the moment, streetcars. Shown are three early 19th century landmarks completed within a decade of each other: Godefroy's Unitarian Church (1820), Washington Monument (1829) and what became in 1877 the Athenaeum Club (1830), a men's club founded by culturally astute Baltimore social register types whose fondness for books and the arts paled beside their fondness for drink. "We were organized for the promotion of literature and the arts," a member once remarked, "but it appears that our only profit has come from our sins and weaknesses." Originally it was the home of William Howard, who purchased the Ionic columns from the Beaver Dam quarries at Cockeysville. The house was razed in 1910. *Pratt*

TURBULENCE: Duplicating early 20th century, middle-of-the-road views is risky business, requiring artful dodging and rear-view vision. Through use of both, the author managed. The office building at northeast corner was erected by C.J. Benson and Company in 1912. It lacks the Athenaeum's Greek revival grandeur, yet maintains a similar symmetry and scale to the Mt. Vernon neighborhood's southern approach. And then there's the Monument, pointing true north like a gigantic compass needle for lifelong suburbanites lost in the maze of downtown streets.

John Eager Howard's bronzed likeness has been perched atop his horse (in foreground) since 1904, watching Charles Street change through the 20th century. The change was abhorred by one Henry Louis Mencken: "With the invasion of Charles Street, above the Monument, by store fronts of protean and appalling hideousness, the old Baltimore bids us goodbye," he wrote in 1929. But the invasion was far from complete, even by the late 1930s. A directory from the period lists in the 800 block (shown) the University Club (at 801), two doctors, two dentists, two hairdressers, one optician, a real estate office and one or two restaurants. Landmarks include the 1912 Latrobe Apartments (Charles and Read Streets) and the elegant 1903 Belvedere Hotel; it ran in the red for part of the decade, yet still retained its status as Baltimore's premier hostelry. *Pratt*

If Mencken was appalled by a few "hideous" storefronts in 1929, we can only guess what he'd say about this block of Charles Street in the mid-1990s. A parking lot had replaced almost half the block's odd side years before (Mencken's beloved Peabody Book Store, one block north, came down in 1997 following a foreclosure) and the invasion of commercialism was complete. Restaurants, including Tony Cheng's at the old University Club, occupied the 1840s-era buildings, among Mt. Vernon's oldest, at the northwest and northeast corners of Charles and Madison. Beginning in late 1992, Donna's, a popular coffee house (probably not a place the untrendy Mencken would have patronized) at the northwest corner (left), drew a large contingent of area residents and suburbanites. Sipping their wine and cappuccino at the sidewalk cafe on warm nights, Donna's patrons turned what had been an uneasy atmosphere into a festive one. The Latrobe was renovated in 1984, while the Belvedere, battered in spirit (after a number of owners and receiverships) but still proud, went condo in 1990.

LOOKING NORTH FROM THE WASHINGTON MONUMENT, 1936

LOOKING NORTH FROM THE WASHINGTON MONUMENT

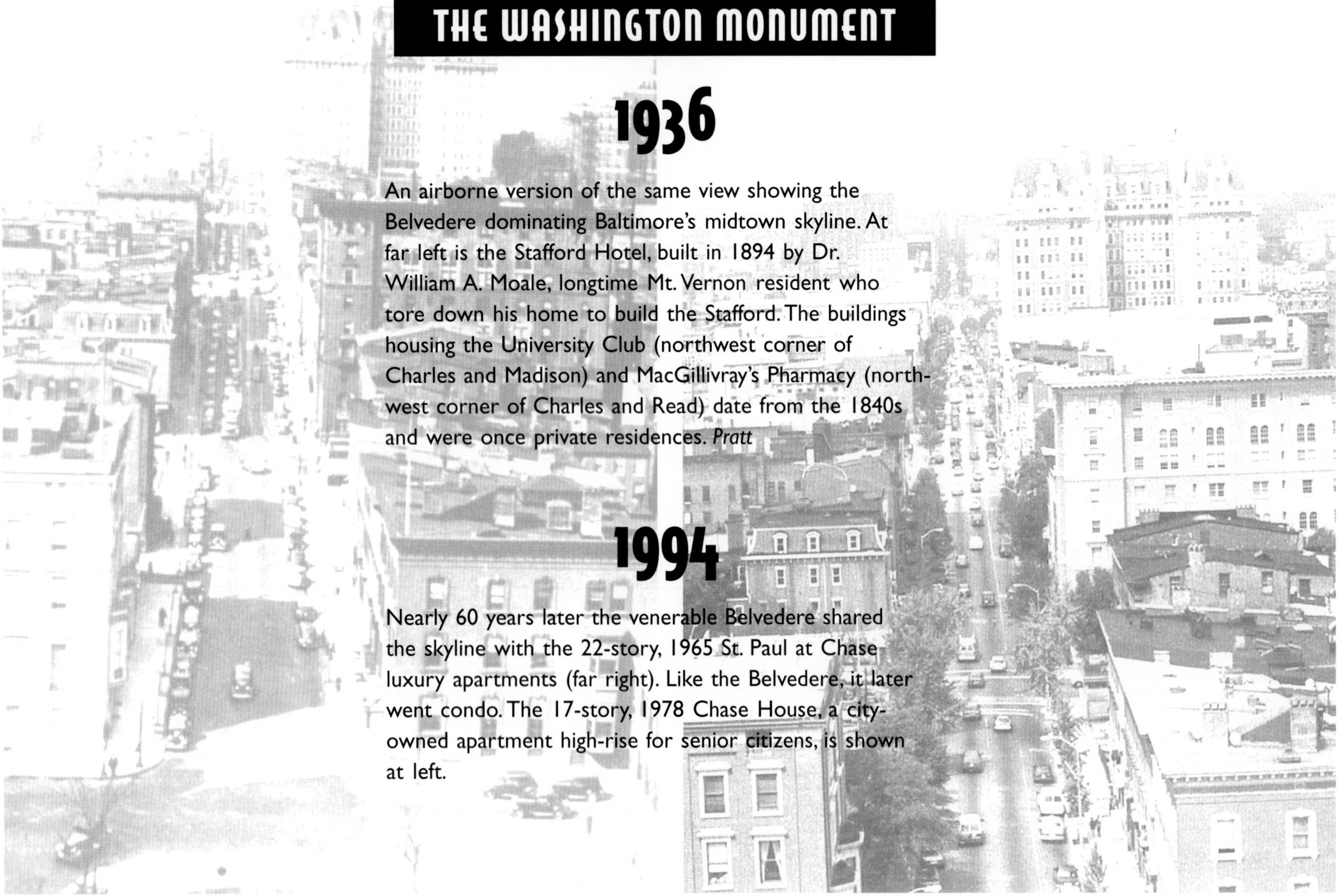

1936

An airborne version of the same view showing the Belvedere dominating Baltimore's midtown skyline. At far left is the Stafford Hotel, built in 1894 by Dr. William A. Moale, longtime Mt. Vernon resident who tore down his home to build the Stafford. The buildings housing the University Club (northwest corner of Charles and Madison) and MacGillivray's Pharmacy (northwest corner of Charles and Read) date from the 1840s and were once private residences. *Pratt*

1994

Nearly 60 years later the venerable Belvedere shared the skyline with the 22-story, 1965 St. Paul at Chase luxury apartments (far right). Like the Belvedere, it later went condo. The 17-story, 1978 Chase House, a city-owned apartment high-rise for senior citizens, is shown at left.

MOUNT ROYAL AVENUE
LOOKING WEST FROM ST. PAUL STREET

1930

GASOLINE ALLEY: In the bygone days of the Zephyr, Hupmobile, DeSoto and Terraplane, Mt. Royal Avenue was surrounded by automobile dealerships, auto parts and tire outlets. The Automobile Club of Maryland was headquartered here, first at the northwest corner of Charles and Mt. Royal, later at the southeast corner of Mt. Royal and Maryland. In the 1930s neighborhood dealerships included Weiss Motor Co., Levi Motors and Monumental Motors. The 1906 building on the northwest corner of Mt. Royal and Charles, originally headquarters for AAA, later did duty as a showroom, roller-skating rink, bowling alley, gymnasium and restaurant. Just behind it is the Lyric Theatre, to many ears considerably less than "acoustically perfect," all the hype notwithstanding. It opened in 1894 and prefaced Mt. Royal's evolution into a cultural district. *Pratt*

1994

CULTURE ALLEY: The Meyerhoff Symphony Hall (1982) and Lyric Opera House (what it became after its major renovation the same year) forged the Mt. Royal area into a true cultural district. The former AAA Building/dealer showroom/skating rink metamorphosed into the University of Baltimore's Academic Center—what some still call "the garage" in deference to its past life—via an exquisite 1971 renovation by the architectural firm of Fisher, Nes, Campbell and Partners. The Sutton Place Apartments (shown behind the old B&O Mount Royal Station tower) at 1111 Park Avenue was considered a classy address when it opened in 1962. Built on the edge of tony Bolton Hill, it still affords in-town luxury apartment living, panoramic views, of course, and easy access to the area's academic and cultural centers. An eclectic mix of tenants—students, retirees, doctors, lawyers, local media celebrities (Cal Shuman, Jim West, Fat Daddy)—have called Sutton Place home. Resident and eccentric inventor (of traffic-activated signal devices) Charles Adler died here in 1980. A man apparently obsessed with peace and quiet, he rented several apartments just to make sure he got it.

(Full size photographs follow)

The Mt. Royal District still beamed from a beautification program dating from the 1890s. The gardens of Mt. Royal Terrace, an ornamented St. Paul Street Bridge (the two women shown at the south end of the bridge, a work by sculptor D.A. Henning, represented truth and justice) and the newly-built Murchison-designed, Beaux-Arts Pennsylvania Station (called Union Station until the late 1920s) lent a spiffy elegance to the place. Once extending to the Jones Falls' northern bank, the gardens proved vulnerable to railroad pollution and were dismantled for additional track space. The station in 1911 replaced the former 1880s Union Station. The seven-story building (1420 N. Charles Street) at left became in 1904 headquarters for the Baltimore Athletic Club. The regal looking (at least for a water pumping station) Mt. Royal Pumping Station, visible in the distance just left of Jones Falls, was built around 1896 and stood at North Avenue and McMechen Street. *Library of Congress*

Like the Fallsway before it, the JFX consigned its namesake to a subterranean existence. Construction of it in 1960 altered the St. Paul Street bridge, stripping it of its fine iron work, including Henning's iron ladies. The gardens disappeared too, supplanted with additional concrete, as did the pumping station. Pennsylvania Station has been under periodic renovation since its construction; the last major face-lift (1983) was a huge $5 million affair (it originally cost $2 million to build) that was expected to restore the station to its former Beaux-Arts grandeur and add momentum to the city's midtown Charles Street revitalization effort. Results can best be described as uneven, reflected in vacant and restored residential property in close proximity. The University of Baltimore in 1947 purchased the old Baltimore Athletic Club building, one of many buildings the University would either purchase or build around Charles and Mt. Royal. By the 1970s, the school had become the most stabilizing force in a district beset with its share of rising street crime and declining commercial investment.

Looking East from the Munsey Building
1937, 1963, 1995

In 1937, urban renewal laid siege to the early 19th century warrens of Old Town. A recently-widened Fayette Street (center) is shown plowing through one of a half dozen neighborhoods designated as slums in W.W. Emmart's classic 1934 study for the Real Estate Board. Emmart didn't mince words; this "ring of blight" surrounding Baltimore's commercial center, he said, should be demolished or at least thinned out. At the time, Front, High, and Exeter Streets between Fayette and Lexington (left), a matrix located just east of St. Vincent's and the Shot Tower, was a curious amalgam of auto parts dealers, clothing stores, mom and pop delicatessens and Jewish residents who had not yet fled to the northwest suburbs. Landmarks include the War Memorial, the 1926 Central District Police Headquarters (just east of it) and Shot Tower. Front and center is the Tower Building.

While never a candidate for the plush and fancy award, the sterile, blocky high-rise complex (designed after the hastily-constructed, European post-war models) of Lafayette Courts, shown here in a sort of marching lockstep, was once reasonably comfortable. Longtime residents speak of a time from the mid-1950s to the early 1960s when violent crime was relatively low, the apartments' plumbing and electricity still worked and "crack" could be a smart aleck remark or something found in cement. Built 1954–1955, the six, 11-story buildings that formed Lafayette Courts, a legacy of the Emmart study, were monuments to a well-intentioned, mid-century urban renewal plan turned sour. They seemed like a good idea at the time—clean, modern, light-filled apartments offering panoramic views for poor blacks relocated from old, decaying

housing stock. Later, after violent crime, municipal neglect and resident vandalism had all but wrecked them, they were dismissed as monuments to racist social engineering, designed to contain and segregate blacks from whites. The Frayer and Associates-designed INA Building (Insurance Company of North America) under construction at lower left was the first office building in 30 years constructed near City Hall. Under new ownership (Two-Twenty-Two Partnership) in 1963, the 1912 Tower Building was undergoing a $300,000 interior renovation designed to fill the building's 30 percent vacancy rate. It worked. Within a year, all available space was rented, no mean feat considering that budding Charles Center offered tenants more modern downtown office space. Twenty-three years later, amid voices of protest, the building came down for a parking lot.

In deference to the times, the city finally demolished Lafayette Courts on 19 August 1995 in a much-heralded media spectacle dubbed "The Implosion." The author's view dates from late November, just after the city had finished clearing the rubble. Pleasant View Gardens, new town homes built on the site, gave the working poor a chance at home ownership. The INA Building (foreground) came down in 1997 for a 500-space parking garage, 250 of those spaces reserved for Alexander Brown Inc. as incentive to keep Brown from relocating its corporate offices to the suburbs. The city's main branch of the 1971 U.S. Post Office, just east of St. Vincent de Paul Church, wreaks of the Brutalist influence. Brutalism reveled in stark, bare slabs of concrete and went out rather quickly. For many, not quickly enough.

**LOOKING EAST FROM
THE MUNSEY BUILDING,**
1937, *Pratt*

**LOOKING EAST FROM
THE MUNSEY BUILDING, 1963,**
Maryland Historical Society

**LOOKING EAST FROM
THE MUNSEY BUILDING,
1995**

FAYETTE STREET LOOKING EAST FROM FRONT STREET, CIRCA 1935

A ground-level view of E. Fayette Street two years before renewal. A December 1937 *Sun* article that supported the Emmart study tossed rag dealers and Afro-Americans into the same socio-economic stew: "Even before Fayette Street was widened that section between the Shot Tower and Broadway was regarded as a blighted neighborhood. Rents were low. Properties were in a bad state of repair. Many storerooms and dwellings were unoccupied. Rag dealers and Negroes were moving in." The photo shows another side of E. Fayette Street, one where commerce thrived on a lively street-scape. The church at left is St. Matthew's German Evangelical Lutheran. Built in 1852, its spire rose 180 feet high and contained three bells captured by German forces during the Franco-Prussian War. *Peale Museum*

FAYETTE STREET LOOKING EAST FROM FRONT STREET, 1994

Urban renewal in 1937 and subsequently, improved traffic flow and perhaps even displaced a few rag dealers. Some of those "negroes" in the early 1940s were relocated into the low rise projects of Lafayette Courts, built two blocks east of what became in 1971 the city's main branch of the United States Post Office (left), a sprawling, $24.1 million edifice designed by Cochran, Stephenson and Donkervoet, Tatar and Kelley. The 1890 four-story building just east of Shot Tower, Dr. Holmes Plating in earlier view, and subsequently longtime home (late 1930s–1977) of Milkmak Candy Factory, housed two restaurants (Schatzie's, Chez Fernand) and a disco before the Pressley Ridge Schools purchased it in fall 1995 for $525,000. The city in the 1980s carved Front Street south of the Shot Tower (right) into a cobblestoned promenade called "museum row," which includes a former mayor's home (9 Front Street).

LEXINGTON STREET LOOKING WEST TOWARD WAR MEMORIAL PLAZA, 1935

TALL, TALLER, TALLEST: Four Baltimore landmarks, Tower Building, Baltimore Trust, Munsey Building and City Hall seem to vie for vertical supremacy in this Depression-era view. When the Munsey was completed in 1911, it was Baltimore's tallest skyscraper. Note the famous Bromo Seltzer bottle nestled between it and the dome of City Hall. The 51-foot high, 17-ton bottle was removed from the Emerson Tower (also completed in 1911) in 1936 (for safety reasons—it wobbled in high winds), and sentimental Baltimoreans have looked forward to its return ever since. The 1925 War Memorial Building (left) stands amid 19th-century residential rowhouse development that was beginning to look out of place in an area shedding its residential character. *Pratt*

LEXINGTON STREET LOOKING WEST TOWARD WAR MEMORIAL PLAZA, 1993

MEASURE FOR MEASURE: In feet, the 590-foot, copper-hued Merritt Tower at 6 St. Paul Street edges out the 500-foot NationsBank Building, designed by a local firm (Taylor and Fisher, Smith and May). In stories, the NationsBank Building reigns supreme, 35 to 28. Actually, dwarfing Baltimore's only art deco skyscraper just might have occurred to the tower's financier, Merritt chief executive Gerald S. Klein. Completed shortly after the 1985 collapse of Merritt Savings and Loan, the tower earned the contempt of critics who called it Klein's "ego trip" and a symbol of the overreaching that led to the failure of the Maryland Savings Share Insurance Corp., a private insurer of savings and loan deposits. Purchased by the state in 1993 for $12.2 million, the tower in the summer of 1994 became one of several structural monuments honoring outgoing Governor William Donald Schaefer (renamed William Donald Schaefer Tower). In 1986, the Parker and Thomas-designed, Beaux-Arts Tower Building earned an entirely different status: Lost Baltimore Landmark.

MARK B. MILLER

LOOKING WEST FROM SHOT TOWER, CIRCA 1910

LOOKING WEST FROM SHOT TOWER, CIRCA 1994

Narrative follows

Looking West from Shot Tower

CIRCA
1910

YEAR
1994

Photographers found Baltimore's only surviving shot tower (the city once had three), erected in 1828, an ideal observatory from which to take panoramic views of the city. The Hughes Company photographer behind this well-preserved image, captured what in the mid-18th century was marshland, citizen Thomas Harrison's property known appropriately as "Harrison's marsh." By the mid-19th century and into the early years of the 20th, it was both a residential and industrial district, punctuated with workers' homes, seedy hotels and factories like the Hess Brothers shoe manufacturing plant (lower left, hugging the south side of Fayette Street) and M.L. Himmell & Son (upper center), a furniture supplier for offices and bowling alleys. Other landmarks of note include, in foreground from left to right, Laverine House, St. Vincent's orphan asylum and St. Vincent's Church (1840). The hipped-roof Church Of The Messiah, seen at upper left of photo, stood on southwest corner of Gay and Fayette, one block east of City Hall. Note in foreground Jones Falls at low tide and just west of it the legendary Harrison Street, known for liquor, second-hand dry goods and dirty water dumped from the Jones Falls in flood mode. A devastating flood in 1906 initiated its decline. By 1925, according to a period *Sunpapers* article, the street's west side had been reduced to "a few old men who still sit and stand—waiting for the trade that rarely comes." By the mid-1930s, a decade after the Central District Police Headquarters had claimed most of the street, a few businesses like Pollack's Uniform and M. Kolker Merchandise survived on Harrison Street between Baltimore and Fayette Streets and north of Lexington Street. *Maryland Historical Society*

In the 1920s, with the dedication of the Memorial Building and City Hall Plaza (1927), Mr. Harrison's once soggy real estate began its metamorphosis from scruffy industrial district to municipal office complex, what became known as the Civic Center. Landmarks include the 1931 Abe Wolman Municipal Building (originally the Hoen Building, just right of City Hall), the 1972 Central District Police Station (southeast corner of Gay and Fayette Streets) and the 1992 Legal Aid Bureau (just right of Memorial Building). The mid-1980s JFX extension sliced off over a block's worth of Lexington Street and turned the Fallsway (right) into an urban backroad of sorts. Grass oval next to southbound lane was site of the 1926 Central District, razed in 1984. Even the name Civic Center proved somewhat evanescent, fading from general use through the decades and associated more with the sporting arena built in conjunction with the Charles Center project. If not for St. Vincent's Church, a designated historial landmark, it would be almost impossible to match this view with its predecessor.

CIRCA 1850

Looking Northwest from Shot Tower

The Washington Monument stands all by its lonesome in this mid-19th century daguerreotype by H.H. Clark. At lower right the Gay Street bridge spans the Jones Falls; at lower left alley-wide, ancient Frederick Street winds northwest into Gay Street; at upper left the domes of the Unitarian Church and Cathedral dominate a skyline still ringed with thick tree growth. Note contrast between the modest, two-story workers' quarters in foreground, situated near slaughter houses and iron foundries, and the gentry's relatively grand, three-story town houses clustered around the Monument. In the days before office towers and high-rise apartment buildings obstructed near-ground-level views of Baltimore's older inner-core, the city's wealthy, perched on higher elevation, could look down, literally as well as figuratively, on their less prosperous neighbors.
Peale Museum

If not for the Washington Monument, a time-traveler from 1850 would be hopelessly lost in this piece of Baltimore that bears almost no resemblance to its antebellum self. The workers' homes and slaughter houses, scraped and burned off the landscape like so many barnacles, have given way to block-sized office buildings, warehouses and parking garages like Quille-Crown's paneled facade, 1950s-era, three-story unit shown on the west side of Guilford Avenue. The Robert Mills-designed, $200,000, 178-foot, lottery-financed marble column preceded the urban byproducts of the automobile age and will most likely survive 21st century urban incarnations and continue to lend a sense of place like no other city landmark before 1829 or since.

YEAR 1996

(Full size photographs follow)

MARK B. MILLER

Looking East from Shot Tower
circa 1850, 1949, 1996

Another H.H. Clark daguerreotype shows a swath of East Baltimore the way Edgar Allen Poe would have seen it—assuming the writer felt the view was worth climbing 215 feet of steps for a look. Poe, who once lived near the Shot Tower, died 7 October 1849 in an infirmary at the Washington College Hospital, the domed 1838 building topped with weather vane (after it became Church Home and Hospital in January 1858, the weather vane was replaced with a cross donated by Old St. Paul's Church). Poe's funeral procession rolled westward on Baltimore Street (far right) to Front Street en route to Westminster burying ground. Multi-acre estates defined much of Washington Hill and the city beyond Broadway. Further west, in foreground, we see Oldtown's antebellum housing stock and the roof of one 1781 building, the Oldtown Meetinghouse at northeast corner of Fayette (left) and Aisquith Streets. Fairmount Avenue (between Fayette and Baltimore), then Little Hamstead Street, extended from Central Avenue eastward to the western edge of George W. Corner's fence-enclosed Washington Hill estate.

Jack Engeman's 1949 view shows East Baltimore's open spaces east of Broadway filled with post-Civil War rowhouse development. Church Home's distinctive gold dome is barely visible among the hospital's subsequent additions. Johns Hopkins Hospital's original building (upper left corner) dates from 1889. Also evident is the industrial and commercial takeover of what a century earlier had been residential space. The smokestacked building in center, built in the early 1890s as a switching station for Baltimore City Passen-

ger Railway, became in 1912 the Hendler's Ice Cream plant. The 1890s-era building in foreground, originally the J. King & Co. horse stables, had become Saval Products' meat-processing plant. Much of the surviving ancient housing stock between Colvin Street and the low-rise projects of Lafayette Courts (upper left) would in a few years be bulldozed for those infamous high-rises. The Old-town Meetinghouse, almost wholly visible in this view and in 1850 fully integrated architecturally into the dense, urban residential aesthetic of that time, was beginning to look quaint among its changing surroundings.

An expanded Johns Hopkins and Church Home, in addition to the 1970 22-story Broadway apartment complex for senior citizens (center), is shown on the horizon. What had been Exeter Street north of Fayette became in 1971 a parking lot entrance ramp (lower left) for the U.S. Post Office building. Soon after the author took this view, construction of Pleasant View Gardens began on lots between Colvin and Aisquith Streets; it opened in October 1997. The old Hendler plant, closed in the mid-1970s, served as offices for a job-training agency. Note at right the 1876 "second Lloyd Street Synagogue." Designed in the Moorish style, it served B'Nai Israel Congregation into the mid-1990s, one of only three Jewish congregations left in the inner city. The Oldtown Meeting-house, fully restored in 1996 as the McKim Center, stands as the only relic from this district's colonial past and one of the few left from the mid-19th century. But note the street pattern: almost fully intact after 146 years.

LOOKING EAST FROM SHOT TOWER, 1949, *PEALE MUSEUM*

DOWN BY THE OLDE MILL STREAM: A deceptively inert Jones Falls flows by St. Vincent de Paul Church. Directly ahead is the Fayette Street bridge. The row homes (right) along Harrison Street were built a couple decades after painter Sir Francis Guy in the early 19th century depicted the stream's banks as bucolic and tranquil and conducive to fishing and picnicking. But even then, "that belligerent little stream," as local author Letitia Stockett aptly put it, was a problem. It flooded frequently during summer rainstorms and Baltimoreans turned it into an open sewer, a stenchy repository for waste and flotsam. Beginning in 1815, the city installed stone retaining walls. The one shown at right might date from the major wall-construction project launched after the devastating flood of July 1868. As early as 1817, planner Benjamin Latrobe had proposed covering the Falls altogether, a proposal revised by others throughout the 19th century, but one that wouldn't become a reality until the 20th. Never mind that the Falls had stopped the 1904 fire in its rampaging tracks, thereby saving East Baltimore. By 1911, Baltimoreans had had enough; it was the year they approved a loan for the Fallsway. *Pratt*

STREET OVER TROUBLING WATERS: "The Fallsway is a hideous object, no matter how beneficent it may be for trade," wrote Ms. Stockett in the late 1920s. She missed the Jones Falls, even its belligerence. "It (Fallsway) will never be like the Falls, a rampaging tawny devil when in flood roaring along under the bridges while fascinated loafers, and a few industrious citizens leaned over the railing wondering—well, wondering whatever people do wonder when they watch swift running water." Completed in 1915, the $2,000,000 Fallsway buried the Jones Falls under tons of concrete. At its dedication, former Mayor Mahool expressed hope that the new road would "wipe out the barrier that for years has separated East Baltimore from West Baltimore." It didn't, at least not psychologically, as the east and west sides of town continued to maintain a regional sensibility throughout the century. Urban renewal, as the view shows, erased everything except St. Vincent's. Straight ahead is Scarlett Place, a 1987 condominium project built on top of an old warehouse. At far right, the stacks of the recycled (and recycled and recycled and recycled) Power Plant.

JONES FALLS LOOKING SOUTH, 1994

GAY STREET LOOKING SOUTHWEST FROM MONUMENT STREET

1890s Gay Street (with telephone poles), along with Monument (foreground) and Aisquith (right) Streets, formed Ashland Square. More triangle than square, it took shape in the early 1800s after the city extended Monument Street east from the Jones Falls. In 1858 the square became the final resting place for Daniel Wells and Henry C. McComas (they were initially interred in Greenmount), teenagers killed in 1814 during the Battle of North Point; the Wells-McComas Monument (foreground), built above their tomb, was dedicated in 1873. Gay Street between Forrest and Monument Streets had long been the commercial hub of Oldtown, sometimes spelled Old Town and earlier known as Jones Town until the 1740s when Nick Ruxton Gay surveyed it just after it merged with its fledgling, slightly older neighbor to the west, Baltimore. Oldtown was largely a German, Irish and Jewish neighborhood (Hochschild's, a dry goods business born on Gay Street in 1836, still had a store there as well as one on Howard Street in the 1890s) in the straw-boater, knicker-era "gay '90s." The view does not show Horn's, an eatery that stood on Monument, just west of Aisquith, where neighborhood boys in the summer would rent wagons and canvass cakes of Horn's famous "Hokey Pokey" ice cream. Perhaps the youngster crossing Monument Street was one such Hokey Pokey pusher himself. *Peale Museum*

1994 By the 1960s, Hokey Pokey pushers had long been supplanted by drug pushers, a grim reflection of Oldtown's precipitous decline after World War Two. Gay Street competed with Pennsylvania Avenue as the meanest, baddest main drag in town, its dubious reputation confirmed when the April 1968 riots started there (rioters struck again during the Blizzard of February 1979, angering an incredulous Mayor Schaefer who thought his administration had improved the quality of life along the Gay Street corridor) following the assassination of Martin Luther King Jr. Because the riots devastated Gay Street, putting some of the merchants there permanently out of business, it has long been assumed that the conflagration became the catalyst for the Gay Street Mall. In fact, the Gay Street Merchants Association had discussed the transit mall concept with city planners a few years before. Completed in 1976, the mall's Phase Two project (from Orleans to Aisquith Streets) was part of the early- to mid-1970s Oldtown urban renewal package funded by $8.8 million in federal grants. The project, at least initially, infused the impoverished area with a sense of pride and hope, the "snow riot" of '79 notwithstanding. The mall's vacancy rate stood at only 10 percent in the late 1970s, then spiraled upward to around 50 percent 20 years later. Stanley Zerden, owner of Queen's Dress Shop and president of the Oldtown Mall Merchants Association, attributes much of the recent, precipitous decline to the loss of Lafayette Courts. In late 1997 Mr. Zerden was "cautiously optimistic" that a proposed supermarket and drug store, coupled with potential business from Pleasant View Gardens, might pull Gay Street out of its economic doldrums. Meanwhile, the obelisk remains as it was back in 1873, while beneath it, as far as we know, Mr. Wells and Mr. McComas continue to rest in peace.

(Full size photographs follow)

GAY STREET LOOKING SOUTHWEST FROM MONUMENT STREET, 1994

FAYETTE AND HOWARD STREETS LOOKING EAST

1906

Jacob Epstein's Baltimore Bargain House forms the backdrop for this lively, early century street scene when straw hats or boaters were all the rage and the Gibson Girl defined the American feminine ideal. Baltimore was almost as famous for its boaters as its seafood, cranking out three-fourths of the nation's supply in an era when a gentleman wasn't considered well-dressed without his head covered. No doubt, the city had its fair share of Gibson ladies, too. Who are those Oliver Hardy look-alikes strolling west on Fayette?
Peale Museum

1994

The Gibson Girl passed on after World War One, boaters after World War Two. Baseball caps, fed by a growing sports mania and worn by the two young men warily eyeing the author's camera, were all the rage by the 1980s. McDonald's arrived on the southeast corner of Howard and Lexington in 1973, some years after construction crews had cut down the Baltimore Bargain House to three stories and turned it into a parking garage.

(Full size photographs follow)

FAYETTE AND HOWARD STREETS LOOKING EAST, 1906

Howard Street Looking North from Lexington Street
1913, 1941, 1995

Howard Street was as much a street as a state of mind. It was the city's Main Street before The Mall, the place where Baltimoreans shopped before they fled the city and that those of a certain age return to in their dreams of Baltimore yesterdays. The district grew from tracts John Eager Howard donated in the 1780s. Businesses were operating on Howard Street as early as 1801. Housed in small, two and three story buildings with dormers and canopies extending from their entrances, they foreshadowed the coming of the Big Four: Abram Hutzler in 1858, Max Hochschild (who teamed up with Louis and Beno Kohn in 1897) in 1870, Louis Stewart in 1901, the May Co. (southwest corner of Howard and Lexington) in the 1920s. Howard and Lexington was the district's commercial hub through the 1960s, the city's heart and soul of retailing, the center of the universe for Baltimore shoppers on Saturday afternoons. The 1913 view shows Hutzler's at left, Stewart's at right; Hochschild's is out of view. Hutzler's 1888 Romanesque, Baldwin and Pennington-designed building replaced the original store. Stewart's building was built by the Posner family in 1899.

In 1941 construction crews (note scaffolding) added five floors to Hutzler's 1932, James R. Edmunds-designed, art deco addition. Hochschild's is shown at far left. Mano Swartz furriers, shown just north of Stewart's, moved to Howard Street from Lexington in 1923. The district's other retail stalwarts between Lexington and Mulberry included Stieff Silversmiths, Hess Shoes, Virginia Dare Restaurant, Mill End Shop, Kwash Furriers, Seifert Engraver's and a novelty shop with a novel name, National Toy Gas Balloon Company. Trackless trolleys succeeded streetcars on Howard Street in the late 1930s.

Main Street remained healthy and vibrant into the 1950s, bathing in the long afterglow of post-war prosperity. Still, the district's loss of retail traffic had already begun, an inevitable consequence of middle-class life shifting outward. The shifting picked up steam through the 1970s and 1980s. Hochschild-Kohn closed in 1977,

Stewart's in 1979, Hecht's (May Co.) and Hutzler's in 1989. Morton's (left), a department store operating out of the old Hochschild's building, made a good go of it from 1989 until it closed in 1997. Some of the specialty shops, cylinders in the street's retail engine even during the heyday of the Big Store, still did respectable business serving a largely inner-city clientele.

Even so, by the early 1990s the district was a commercial backwater limping on into an uncertain future. The arches, installed by the city about 1984, proved to be so much hollow razzmatazz, a feckless municipal spruce-up effort. Restricting automobile traffic between Fayette and Franklin Streets beginning in the late 1980s didn't help much either. The city had hoped that foot traffic alone and the proposed Light Rail system (note tracks) would infuse the moribund district with new life. It didn't. Merchants complained that few of the 18,600 (as of 1993) city-bound, Light Rail riders were stopping to shop on Howard Street. Their collective sentiment: Dump the transit mall and bring back the automobiles. In September 1996 the Schmoke administration did just that, basing its decision on a report by the Howard Street Task Force empathetic to the merchants. A year later one area merchant informed the author that business was on the upswing in what some had derisively called "Death Valley."

Others talked more optimistically about a "new," revitalized Howard Street. Groups like the Downtown Partnership of Baltimore, Economics Research Associates, Baltimore Development Corporation and the West Side Task Force, a group formed in late 1997 by representatives of the Harry and Jeanette Weinberg Foundation (which owns much of the district's real estate), commissioned studies and dreamed big dreams. Howard Street could become an artists' colony, or a neighborhood of young professionals and students, or a high-tech center for computer and research labs, or a district of quasi-government agencies like Lochheed-Martin (headquartered in Hutzler's old Palace building, it was hired by the city to collect back child support), or even a more viable retail district with stores that would work for the area. Few group members harbored sentimental illusions about Howard Street returning as it was. A second golden age was possible, they felt. But it would be different.

1913

1941

HOWARD STREET LOOKING NORTH FROM LEXINGTON STREET, 1941, *PRATT*

1995

CRITICAL MASS (ABOVE): Christmas is in the air (note Santa-clad women in foreground), but the mobs have gone to Towson, White Marsh, Owings Mills, Columbia and elsewhere. Many of the people seen here are on their way to Lexington Market. Of the Lexington Street stores from 1930, Woolworth's won the longevity award; it hung on through the decades before closing in the mid-1990s. Like Howard Street, Lexington became the domain of specialty shops catering to inner-city residents and bargain-minded suburbanites that worked downtown. In the late 1990s Lexington Street between Howard and Liberty claimed a spate of second-hand clothing stores (Young World, New York Fashions, Cityzone, Private Label, New York Variety, Index), three shoe stores (Footlocker, Pic & Pay, Payless), a jeweler (Bliss), CVS Pharmacy, Wig House and other retail concerns, many of them Korean-owned. Howard and Lexington, while no longer the city's epicenter of retailing, remained far from dead.

MASS DENSITY (LEFT): It's beginning to look a lot like Christmas . . . Howard and Lexington was always mobbed around the Christmas holidays, depression or no depression. Wrote Mary Fisher in 1933: "Long ago Howard Street traded yesteryear's gentle speech for the gentle patter of price tags; its heart is a cash register and its soul is the jam of shoppers at Lexington and Howard on Saturday afternoon." Ask those shoppers what they miss most about the old Howard and Lexington at Christmas and many of them will tell you the magnificent window displays, especially the ones at Hutzler's. Lexington Street between Howard and Liberty featured Mitchell Fur Co., Gutman's, Tuerke Baggage, F.W. Woolworth, W.T. Grant, S.S. Kresge, Stanwick's, Forsythe Shoes, Wilson Shoes, Michelson Hat Shop and Schulte-United Department Store. *Peale Museum*

WEST LEXINGTON STREET LOOKING WEST FROM LIBERTY STREET, 1931

LEXINGTON STREET LOOKING WEST FROM LIBERTY STREET, 1996

The New, the block's last theatre, moved around the corner to Park Avenue in 1967. Save for the reassuring presence of police vehicles, the block has remained car-free since its renovation into a suburban-type pedestrian mall. Dedicated 21 June 1974, the mall was one of many installed during the 1970s in other Eastern cities that, like Baltimore, tried to halt the decline of once prosperous retail districts by closing streets off to automobile traffic. By extending the mall from the Charles Center urban renewal area, planners hoped to infuse ailing Howard Street with rich blood pumped from the city's new corporate heart. The mall didn't do much for Howard Street, but Lexington Street retailers like Payless Shoes, Peanut Shoppe, Lane Bryant, Wig House and Index picked up business from the hungry hordes that descend on Lexington Market at lunchtime. The block's late 19th century commercial buildings have remained intact. Note mid-1970s, marbled facade renovation on Modern Mode (105 W. Lexington, third from left).

1931 (LEFT): Another Depression-era look at the hubbub and ballyhoo that was Lexington Street when Jean Harlow and Greta Garbo were queens of the silver screen. By 1931, three years after Warner Brothers released the first all-talking picture ("Lights of New York"), 83 percent of American movie houses were equipped for sound. The New, at 210 W. Lexington, opened in December 1910 as a vaudeville theatre. Morris A. Mechanic bought it from the Whitehurst chain in 1929. *Maryland Historical Society*

The long-awaited $2,500,000 Howard Street extension was nearing completion, an engineering marvel that involved extending Howard Street from the old Richmond Market, tunneling under Mt. Royal Avenue and installing a new bridge over Jones Falls and the Pennsylvania Railroad to North Avenue. A WPA project surfaced Howard Street with red brick. Mayor Howard W. Jackson officially opened it on 12 January 1939, four years after the Wyatt and Nolting-designed Fifth Regiment Armory (left) was rededicated following a spectacular 11-alarm fire on 13 January 1933 that destroyed all but the original 1903 building's massive stone walls. Sonja Henie brought her Ice Review here and was hit with a law suit (she was later found not liable) by spectators injured in the famous bleacher collapse of 6 March 1952. *Pratt*

Subsequent area landmarks include Sutton Place (1962) and the Baltimore Life Insurance Building (1960), vacated in 1992 when the company moved to Owings Mills. City and state officials have long considered converting it into a performing arts center, a move that would add yet another cultural anchor to the Mt. Royal district. Sutton Place lost some swank through the years, yet managed to retain its status as one of the city's finer high-rise apartment buildings. Swank cost a lot less in the Sutton's early 1960s heyday: Rents ranged from $150–$250 ($500–$750, late 1990s). Light Rail and the State Center metro afford resident commuters mass transit at their doorstep. Unlike the condemned Baltimore Arena, the stalwart, highly functional Fifth Regiment Armory isn't going anywhere soon. In addition to its chief function as headquarters for the Maryland National Guard, it regularly hosts dog and cat shows, sporting events and the city's annual Oktoberfest. Fires, once a plague upon this place (the January 1933 blaze was just one of many), haven't been a problem since 1959.

Lexington Market (left) was already a century old when an unknown photographer braved an oncoming horsecar to take this view. The generous John Eager Howard, one of George Washington's sidekicks during the Revolution, donated the tract that turned into a farmer's produce market that in turn became one of the most impressive urban food emporiums in the United States. Merchants first enclosed the market in 1803 with a wooden shed that later extended from Paca to Lexington Streets. *Peale Museum*

A 1949 six-alarm fire that destroyed $2 million in property brought the Market's wooden shed era to a resounding end. The city housed the stalls under brick in 1952. Shown here is a portion of the $5.2 million Arcade designed by Baltimore architects Mark Beck Associates, Inc. that opened in October 1982. "A lot of glass—and a touch of class," is how a *Sunpapers* article by critic Elisabeth Stevens described it then. A lot of grime—and a touch of crime is what it became in recent years, with borderline-sanitary eating and restroom facilities, occasional vermin problems and a well-publicized shooting involving a policeman and a young man wielding a knife. Yet for many gastronomes, there will never be anything quite like Lexington Market, a lunchtime circus mobbed by University of Maryland personnel, downtown office workers, West Baltimore residents and tourists who find it hard to resist this place of good and plenty.

100 BLOCK OF EUTAW STREET LOOKING NORTH TOWARD LEXINGTON STREET, 1994

Madison Street Looking West From Park Avenue

1873

THREE WHO DARED . . .

Construction crews were completing the 273-foot main spire of the First and Franklin Presbyterian Church. Dedicated in 1859 upon completion of the main building, the church was designed by a one N.G. Starkwether, an Oxford graduate who dreamed of launching a Gothic revival in the United States. Author George W. Howard wrote this about it in *The Monumental City*: "The ornamentation though simple is highly wrought and the perfect symmetry and grace of its numerous spires, and in fact every portion of the edifice will challenge comparison with any similar effort at home or abroad."

A local photographer hauled himself and his bulky equipment onto the scaffolding and took panoramic views of what is perhaps the most inclusive photographic record of late 19th century Baltimore available. But which local photographer? Most historical sources credit the photos, 13 views in all, to William H. Weaver, who maintained an elaborate photography studio on East Baltimore Street. But in an August 1956 article for the *Evening Sun*, reporter Colin Maclachlan makes no mention of Weaver in Maclachlan's account of how, during a steeple cleaning, Maclachlan followed in the photographer's footsteps, climbed the scaffolding and took his own panoramic views. Maclachlan suggests that a Joseph E. Henry might have shot the 1873 views. "It is assumed that the photographs were taken by Mr. Henry himself although there is no direct evidence of this fact in the file of the Pratt Library," he wrote.

The assumption was based on Maclachlan's vague reference to a story he picked up from equally vague sources. As the story goes, after Henry died in 1937, these unidentified sources, presumably relatives, found the photos and turned them into the Pratt Library. And then there's the corollary story about how architect Edmund G. Lind, N.G. Starkwether's assistant who supervised the steeple's completion in February 1874, allegedly salvaged Henry's photos from the 1904 fire, carrying out 100 pounds of negatives from a downtown photography studio shortly before flames engulfed it. But what studio? Mr. Maclachlan fails to make clear whether it belonged to Henry or Lind. The 1904 Polk City Directory identifies a Joseph E. Henry as an electrical contractor (an electrical engineer in Maclachlan's article) with a business address in the 500 block of West Franklin Street, an area the fire didn't touch. And Lind? The 1904 Polk makes no mention of him.

Either Mr. Henry took his own views or he and/or his relatives gave credit where none was due. Then again, this could simply be a case of limited research by Mr. Maclachlan, who apparently never heard of William H. Weaver, the photographer many have credited for capturing those splendid bird's-eye views of the city in 1873. The author,

without sufficient evidence to the contrary, will also credit Mr. Weaver.

What follows is a clockwise sequence of panoramic steeple views shot by three photographers: Weaver, Maclachlan and Scott McCash, who in 1987 took his own views afforded by another steeple cleaning. The prints show how dramatically inner-city Baltimore changed over the course of 114 years, particularly between 1873 and 1956. The early views show a city no one alive today remembers, a horse-and-buggy city of narrow, semi-paved, tree-lined streets drifting through time in a sort of hushed stillness. It was a city cluttered and dense at its residential inner-core, hungry for more space and on course politically to get it. Colin Maclachlan's mid-century prints show a pace of life quickened and an urban landscape redrawn—mostly, of course, by the internal combustion engine. It was a city widening its main arteries and constructing more parking lots to accommodate more automobiles, losing much of its Victorian architectural legacy (without much preservationist sentiment to save it) to urban renewal and a middle-class trickling out to the suburbs. The city Scott McCash recorded in 1987 mirrored the city of 1956 in accelerated form. Municipal street-widening projects, the commercialization of once-residential areas, the demolition of smaller buildings for bigger, taller buildings and urban flight continued unabated into the 1990s.

LOOKING NORTH FROM FIRST AND FRANKLIN PRESBYTERIAN CHURCH, 1873

LOOKING NORTH FROM FIRST AND FRANKLIN PRESBYTERIAN CHURCH, 1987

1873

1956

1987

Weaver's views followed a post-Civil War building boom that produced 3,500 new houses during the boom's peak years, 1870–1872. The city needed lebensraum, space to breathe and expand. In 1873 those "old placid rows" were creeping toward North Avenue (also known as Boundary or Northern Avenue), then the city's northern boundary. Antebellum estates like "Cloverdale" inhabited the woodsy, still-rural county beyond. The Mount Royal Reservoir (upper left), completed just after the Civil War, beautified the entrance to Druid Hill Park, a 640 acre manor acquired by the city 13 years earlier from the Rogers clan. Businesses housed in early 19th century buildings (left) lined Richmond Street (later Read Street) some 90 years before the psychedelic, Bead Experience era. Tyson Alley, Tyson Street and Howard Street (note horse just north of Tyson Street) cross an undeveloped Park Avenue. The Bolton Depot, where Lincoln embarked on his way to give the Gettysburg Address, is shown just north of where Park Avenue angles sharply left. Merchant-squire George Grundy's circa 1800 Bolton estate lies hidden behind the patch of trees at upper left.

Urban renewal (a term coined by the late James Rouse), not lebensraum, was the buzz word of the mid-1950s. Homes south and west of the Fifth Regiment Armory, site of the old Bolton estate, were being demolished for the new State Office complex. Victorian remnants like the 1888 Romanesque Revival-style Deutches Haus (just north of Park Avenue), originally Bryn Mawr School, were left alone, at least for the time being. Just south of Read Street, what had been modest workers' homes in Weaver's day, awaited the coming of urban pioneers who would restore and gentrify them. Other early 20th century buildings include the Maryland Institute (1906), shown just north of the Armory and west of Howard Street. The B&O's Mt. Royal Station (with clock tower shown to the right of the institute), dedicated in 1896, was still in use after 61 years. The Bolton Depot was gone by the turn of the century, the Mt. Royal Reservoir by 1930, a time when blocks and blocks of Baltimore's old placid rows had been built above North Avenue, leaving Druid Hill Park the nearest big open space at mid-century.

The Joseph Meyerhoff Symphony Hall, so conspicuous in the McCash view, was designed by Pietro, Belluschi, Inc. and Jung-Brannen Associates. It opened in 1982 with great fanfare that included a TV special hosted by Tony Randall. Its quirky design aside (a lopsided wedding cake comes to mind), the hall is an acoustic gem that enriched Baltimore's cultural life, luring urban emigrés back into the city, if only for a few hours. The turreted, 1882 Brexton Apartments at Tyson Street and Park Avenue gained fame as one of many places Wallis Warfield lived during her relatively impoverished Baltimore childhood. It closed in the 1980s and stayed boarded through 1998, its fate in the hands of owners unsure of what to do with it. Note a widened Cathedral Street linked with Park Avenue and the absence of the Deutches Haus, a major casualty sacrificed for the Meyerhoff. But the B&O's Mt. Royal Station survived, thanks to its purchase by the Maryland Institute in 1964, three years after it closed. Sutton Place, shown just north of the armory, opened a few years before young entrepreneurs revitalized Read Street, turning what had been industrial concerns and private residences in 1956 into boutiques like Que Pasa, Hell Bent For Leather and the Bead Experience. In 1987, over a decade after the Bead had moved uptown, the boutiques were struggling to keep customers who had either moved away or spent less time in the city. The Clothes Horse, perhaps the granddaddy of Read Street boutiques dating from at least 1956, closed out its long run in 1997.

Photos courtesy of First and Franklin Presbyterian Church

1873

1956

1987

Weaver swung his lens slightly to the right and recorded the Mt. Vernon district's north side and the zigzag, patch-quilt look of Baltimore's fast-changing, north-central suburban fringe. The extension of old streets, the creation of new ones and rowhouse construction were redefining the aesthetic of this corner of the city. Rowhouse development conformed to uneven construction patterns as shown by isolated residential units like the 1850s-era row of eight fronting Biddle Street (center) and the row of six fronting on Chase a block south. Industries like the Smith & King Sash Factory, the elongated building just west of the Biddle Street row, operated nearby. Park Avenue, Read and Eager Streets form the oblong block in foreground. From left to right, Cathedral Street, Maryland Avenue and Charles Street run parallel through the changing urban mosaic. Union Station's newly-completed first edition is shown just east of Charles and north of a still-undeveloped Jones Falls stream valley. The 1853, $145,000 Maryland Institute for the Blind (top center) stood by itself ("beautifully located," according to *The Monumental City*) on North Avenue, a marble edifice that in 20 years would be surrounded by a grid of rowhouse development built along an extended St. Paul and Calvert Streets. It was torn down around 1905 to make way for the Baltimore Polytechnic Institute.

Save for widened streets and the addition of commercial buildings like the 1923 automobile showroom (Jack Pry Ltd. in 1956) at northeast corner of Cathedral and Eager, much of Mt. Vernon-Belvedere's north

side remained structurally intact from its 1870s-era guise. The early to mid-19th century-era row homes on both sides of Cathedral Street between Eager and Chase, the eclectic row hugging the northeast side of Read and Park and the 1890s-era Queen Anne-style row houses (foreground) filling what had been vacant space in 1873 lent a sense of cohesiveness and community. Note Pennsylvania Station and Baltimore Polytechnic where the Maryland Institute once stood. Extensive landscaping had long since graded what in 1873 had been a steep, barren incline between the Jones Falls stream valley and North Avenue.

Thirty years of commercialization and extensive urban renewal, for better or worse, destroyed much of the Mount Royal district's residential character. Here, it looks more like a place people visit or pass through. Cathedral Street cut a wide swath through what had been Park Avenue north of Biddle; the Meyerhoff Symphony Hall supplanted the Deutches Haus and surrounding neighborhood; the fortress-like Waxter Center (1974) filled space where those rows of Queen Annes once stood. The 1923 automobile showroom, much deteriorated in this photo, would soon be renovated by Schamu, Machowski and Doo Associates into office space and the City Cafe which opened on the first floor in 1995. Remnants from 1873 include 9–15 W. Chase Street (just right of Chase House), the seven Cathedral Street rowhouses between the former showroom and Chase House and at least one house (hidden by Chase House) from that elegant row of eight that commanded center stage in Weaver's photo.

LOOKING NORTH BY NORTHEAST FROM FIRST AND FRANKLIN PRESBYTERIAN CHURCH, 1873

LOOKING NORTH BY NORTHEAST FROM FIRST AND FRANKLIN PRESBYTERIAN CHURCH, 1956

LOOKING NORTH BY NORTHEAST FROM FIRST AND FRANKLIN PRESBYTERIAN CHURCH, 1987

1873, 1956, 1987

Weaver captured the dignified elegance of the Mt. Vernon district in all its late 19th century glory. At lower left, Monument and Cathedral Streets intersect at the west end of West Mount Vernon Place. The circa 1860 Louis Long-designed Garrett mansion (with cupola), home to B&O president John W. Garrett (Garrett willed it to his daughter Mary), stands at southwest corner. It had been just a year since Garrett's son Robert married socialite Mary Sloan Frick. The couple's house, 11 West Mt. Vernon Place, is third building east (left) from Cathedral. The free-spending Mary Sloan Frick Garrett would later acquire numbers 9 and 7 (about one-third of number 7 is visible here) and hire architects Stanford White and John Russell Pope to create one magnificent mansion. One magnificent hotel, the Gothic spiked and spired Saint James (left-center) at southwest corner of Centre and Charles, was just three years old. Past it, the more modest, hipped-roof dwellings of the city's proletariat slope southeast toward a still unfinished City Hall.

Mr. Machlachlan aimed his lens slightly more to the west and south than his predessor, capturing a sliver of Park Avenue (lower right) and less of Monument Street. Shown in foreground is the Mt. Vernon Apartments where the Garrett House stood until the late 1920s. The YMCA building (center), built around 1909, claimed at the northeast corner of Cathedral and Franklin a circa 1820 house attributed to architect Benjamin Latrobe. Shown in Weaver's view, it then served as the Maryland Club. Buildings once inhabited by single families like the town homes just north of the YMCA had been chopped up into apartments and offices. Note Central

Branch of the Pratt Library and, just north of it, the Robert Cary Long-designed Franklin Street Presbyterian Church (1847). The dome of City Hall had longed ceased to dominate Baltimore's skyline, no matter from which direction one viewed it. For sheer altitude, the 34-story Mathieson Building had no peer and wouldn't for another two decades. 300 St. Paul Place (originally Commercial Credit, it became the Fidelity and Deposit Company in late 1980s) is shown under construction just right of the C&P Telephone Building. The venerable Saint James, barely visible behind the Walters Art Gallery and Mt. Vernon Apartments, was sliding into its last decade as one of Mt. Vernon's most endearing landmarks.

The handiwork of Stanford White and John Russell Pope on numbers 7, 9 and 11 West Mt. Vernon Place is evident here. Mrs. Garrett, widowed in 1896, married Dr. Henry Barton Jacobs six years later, then acquired and demolished number 7 West and hired architect Pope to complete her dream house, home to the Engineering Society of Baltimore since 1961. The Peabody Court Hotel, showing recent alterations from its apartment-era guise, blocks view of the Walters' 1974 west wing. The Saint James tumbled in the 1960s for Westminster House (1968) senior citizens home, a nondescript, prosaic design for some, an eyesore for others who had admired what it replaced. The 1890s-era, seven-story Rochambeau (just south of Unitarian Church) apartment building stands on site where General Comte Donatien de Rochambeau and thousands of French troops encamped in July and August of 1782 almost a year after their meeting with Lord Cornwallis at Yorktown. An enthralled, grateful city never forgot.

LOOKING SOUTHEAST FROM FIRST AND FRANKLIN PRESBYTERIAN CHURCH, 1873, *PRATT*

LOOKING SOUTHEAST FROM FIRST AND FRANKLIN PRESBYTERIAN CHURCH, 1956, *PRATT*

1873, 1956, 1987

Park Avenue (center) north of Madison in 1873 was almost exclusively residential, with the accent on *exclusive*. Although it would never rival the pomp and grandeur of New York's Park Avenue, at least 40 families listed in the Baltimore Society Directory (Park Avenue residents listed in society directories up to around 1888 lived north of Centre Street, beyond what became Chinatown. Before then, the city's street numbering was in a state of schizophrenic chaos. The prominent Baldwin family, for instance, listed in 1878 at 105 Park Avenue actually resided at what became number 717 after the system was overhauled) lived on this shaded street in houses sporting roomy interiors and carriage houses in the rear. Enoch Pratt, the quintessential 19th century industrialist/philanthropist, lived here. Pratt's 1847 house on the southwest corner of Park and Monument is shown with its newly-constructed fourth floor designed by architect Edmund G. Lind. A Baltimorean since 1831, Pratt made his seed money in nails and horseshoes before branching out into banking and transportation. Weaver took this view a year after Pratt gained controlling interest in the Maryland Steamboat Co. The Robert Cary Long-designed 1845 St. Alphonsus Catholic Church (Park and Saratoga) towers in the distance. Two blocks south of St. Alphonsus, on 25 July 1873, Baltimore's greatest fire up to that time began at Park and Clay Streets, reputed to be the city's red light district, and spread westward, destroying an entire area between Lexington and Saratoga Streets, Park Avenue and Howard Street. Poor detail in background makes it difficult to tell if Weaver's views preceded or came after the fire.

Enoch Pratt died in 1896 at "Tivoli," his country home near Govans, 10 years after his greatest endowment, the Enoch Pratt Free Library opened on Mulberry Street. The successor to that building, the 1933 Friz, Tildon and Githens-designed main branch is shown here, hogging the block bounded by Cathedral, Franklin and Mulberry Streets. Only the distinctive mansard roof of Pratt's house, much renovated and home to the Maryland Historical Society since 1919, is visible (roof of Mt. Vernon Apartments blocks view of the building's east side) in Machlachlan's photo. A few blocks south, the 300 and 400 blocks of Park Avenue had become known as Baltimore's Chinatown (Shang Wah Long Co., White Rice Inn, China Doll Restaurant, Kung Wo Chong chinaware, etc.), although there was very little to it when compared with the Chinatowns of San Francisco, New York and even Washington, D.C. Block-sized buildings like Hoshschild Kohn's warehouse and the Greyhound Bus Terminal sprawled over lots once reserved for residential units. St. Alphonsus' 30 foot spire, so prominent in background of Weaver's view, is dwarfed here by 20th century buildings like the 21-story Baltimore Gas and Electric headquarters, Lord Baltimore Hotel, B&O Building and Mathieson Building.

Two office/residential towers dominate the foreground in Scott McCash's photo: 611 Park Avenue and Centre Towers. Washington D.C.-based architect Anthony Campitelli designed the upscale, 1966 12-story 611 Park Avenue shown on the street's east side just south of Monument. The Centre Towers, a low- to mid-rent building, at southeast corner of Park and Centre, opened in 1964. Poor management and other problems sent the building into a downward spiral; as of late 1997 it stood vacant, awaiting renovation from new owners. Towers of later vintage, including Two Charles Center, block views of the Maryland National Building and other early century landmarks. Old St. Alphonsus Church appears as a dim beacon to a distant past, fading into the rising verticality of downtown. Subsequent additions to the Maryland Historical Society include the 1982 France-Merrick wing (far right) and the 1967 Thomas and Hugg Memorial wing, just to its left.

LOOKING SOUTH FROM FIRST AND FRANKLIN PRESBYTERIAN CHURCH, 1956, *PRATT*

Photos courtesy of First and Franklin Presbyterian Church

1873

1956

1987

Howard Street is shown with two of its landmarks then under construction: City College, at the southwest corner of Howard and Centre Streets and the Academy of Music, just south of it. After multiple renovations and incarnations, the building just south of the Academy, then the Natatorium gymnasium, would become the Mayfair theater in 1941. Note an alley-wide Centre Street and commercial buildings (showing canopies over their entrances) two blocks south. Hutzler Brothers' small, modest store stood among the nebulous mass of buildings shown here, some 15 years before the debut of their Palace store. The wall-enclosed garden of the Baltimore Academy of the Visitation sits just south of 1850s-era Monument Street rowhouses (foreground). Steeple (far right) of 1852 Westminster Church at Fayette and Green Streets holds a commanding presence in the distance.

The Italianate style City College building (Western High School, 1954–1967), two movie palaces, the Stanley and Mayfair, and Hutzler's Depression-era addition served as Howard Street landmarks into 1956. The Stanley, just left of Western, constructed from remnants of the old Academy of Music, opened in the late 1920s. The 1941 Greyhound Bus Terminal stands on site of the Academy of the Visitation. The Little Tower restaurant (just north of Western) was in its heyday as a hamburger haven around the time a man named Ray Kroc bought out two brothers named McDonald and changed the world with his own burger franchise. Duckpin bowling, also in its heyday, drew patrons to duckpin

bowling centers like Recreation Bowling Alleys, located on the ground floor of the five-story 1926 multi-purpose office building shown just north of Little Tower. The Senator Liquor Store and Hotel, shown next-door, was one of a number of grungy-class establishments the city in later years could have used more of. On the horizon from left to right: Bromo Seltzer Tower (1911), University Hospital (1934) and Montgomery Ward, which opened at Washington Boulevard and Monroe Street in 1925.

In 30 years, structural change on Howard Street was minimal when compared with aggressive development southwest of it. The University of Maryland academic and hospital complex, which seemed to expand exponentially from the 1970s through 1990s, and the 1980 Social Security Administration's Metro West buildings (far right) dominate the southwest skyline. Three landmarks got recycled: The old City College/Western High became the Chesapeake Commons Apartments in 1985; Greyhound (it moved its operations to the I-95 Travel Plaza in 1987) became a government building in 1990 after a hard-fought battle by preservationists to save it; and the old duckpin bowling center became offices for Planned Parenthood. Outpaced by McDonald's and other burger emporiums, the Little Tower closed in the late 1980s. The gap between the old Mayfair (it closed in1986 and remained boarded as of 1998) and Chesapeake Commons is where the Stanley used to be. Its demolition in 1965 for a parking lot symbolized the bygone era of movie palaces. "Oliver" was its last picture show.

LOOKING SOUTHWEST FROM FIRST AND FRANKLIN PRESBYTERIAN CHURCH, 1956

LOOKING SOUTHWEST FROM FIRST AND FRANKLIN PRESBYTERIAN CHURCH, 1987

LOOKING WEST FROM FIRST AND FRANKLIN PRESBYTERIAN CHURCH

1873  **1956**  **1987**

Inner-city, post-Civil War West Baltimore was jampacked with early 19th century housing stock. The modest two and three story dwellings stood shoulder to shoulder along Mary's, Orchard, Biddle, Mootes, Terrier and Elder Streets (Mootes, Terrier and Elder were alley streets), the cluttered matrix shown just west of Eutaw Street, much of it occupied by black residents segregated from main street housing. Annie M. Adams, John Loury, John Henson, Ellias McDonald and Lucretia Alles were among the area's "colored persons" listed in Woods's Baltimore Directory of 1873. The horse and carriage (bottom, center) is crossing the intersection of Madison and Eutaw, perhaps en route to pick up ice from the Melrose Ice Co. The church shown a half block to the northwest is St. Mary's Livery, wedged between Orchard Street and St. Mary's Lane. The spacious grounds of another St. Mary's, St. Mary's Seminary, is shown at upper left (note patch of trees), founded on this site in 1791.

Decompression in the form of commercialization and demolition is evident in the Maclachlan view. Parking lots like the one shown at Madison Street and Linden Avenue, and block-sized buildings like Archer Laundry (with smokestack) and the teens-era Samuel Coleridge Taylor School (upper right) broke up the clutter. The old St. Mary's Livery Church survived into 1956, greatly altered. The neighborhood's thinning out brought into focus landmarks like

the Orchard Street Methodist Church (shown just above Archer's smokestack), founded in 1837 by slaves and freed blacks. First built around 1840, it was rebuilt in 1859 and 1882; in 1992 it became headquarters for the Baltimore Urban League.

By 1987, there was little left of what William Weaver saw in 1873. Fragments of it existed in Seton Hill (shown south and east of the Orchard Street Church), a 1960s-1970s urban restoration project undertaken by urban pioneers, and along the south side of Madison Street. Parking lots like Maryland General Hospital's multi-storied garage (right) took their usual toll. Orchard Mews, a late 1970s townhouse project shown east and west of the church, proved that urban renewal could produce something functional *and* aesthetically pleasing if done right, and Orchard Mews was. Impoverished residents displaced by renewal often ended up in high rise projects like the early 1960s era samples shown just west of Martin Luther King Boulevard. The Orchard Street Church, no longer camouflaged by earlier development, stands out in bold relief among the modern, glass and brick townhomes. The old Archer Laundry fell to a mid-1970s municipal "rechanneling" project, part of the city's ongoing arterial angioplasty that linked a widened and extended Madison Street with McCulloh. Martin Luther King Boulevard, completed about 1980, cut its own swath through what had long become a place suburban commuters passed through and ignored.

LOOKING NORTH BY NORTHWEST FROM FIRST AND FRANKLIN PRESBYTERIAN CHURCH, 1873, *PRATT*

(Narrative follows)

LOOKING NORTH BY NORTHWEST FROM FIRST AND FRANKLIN PRESBYTERIAN CHURCH, 1956, PRATT

LOOKING NORTH BY NORTHWEST FROM FIRST AND FRANKLIN PRESBYTERIAN CHURCH, 1987, *FIRST AND FRANKLIN PRESBYTERIAN CHURCH*

1873 Richmond Market—it looks somewhat like an airplane hangar shoved up against a mid-19th century mansion—established at this site in the early 1830s, dominates Weaver's 1873 view. Located out on what was then (1830s) the city's northwest frontier, the market 40 years later sat amidst a congested residential district. Contiguous arteries shown include Howard (foreground), Biddle (one block west), Eutaw (running diagonally at far left) Streets and Linden Avenue (one block east of Eutaw). The newly-completed (1871) Thomas Walter-designed Eutaw Place Baptist Church (upper left) stands at Eutaw and Dolphin Streets. Soon, stately mansions and townhouses would go up just a few blocks north of it, most notably along Eutaw Place, a choice address for the city's wealthy Jewish merchant and professional class.

1956 Richmond Market's popularity peaked about 1910, when it claimed over 500 stalls. Those were the days when housewives, accompanied by their butlers, would come down and purchase sirloin at 25 cents a pound. By 1937 the market was but 60 percent occupied, a situation city planners hoped the Howard Street extension would improve. The improvement, if there was one, was short-lived: Maclachlan's lens captured the market (sans its cupola) when National Guard units, not food vendors, occupied most of its space. "Now we have to deliver out to the suburbs where everybody lives," lamented one vendor in 1955. Most of the Jewish community had left the Eutaw Place corridor for upper Park Heights: The Sperry-designed 1893 Eutaw Place Temple (Oheb Shalom), its dome shown at center, would be sold to the Prince Hall Masons in 1961. Note on Howard Street the just-completed new building of Maryland General Hospital and the vacant lot where the state would soon begin construction of its new office complex, 301 W. Preston Street.

1987 The 19th century town houses across the street from Howard Street's famed "antique row" were bulldozed to make way for Maryland General's expansion northward. In the mid-1970s the hospital integrated into its complex the old Richmond Market, once a target of the proposed, dreaded and ultimately defeated East-West Expressway. The sun-splashed Maryland State office complex buildings—301 (left) and 201 W. Preston, completed late 1950s and early 1970s respectively—supplanted rows of early 19th century housing stock shown in Weaver's view. Block-sized parking lots stretch along the west side of a widened Eutaw Street long stripped of its Victorian remnants. Scott McCash took in five blocks of early 1940s low-rise housing projects developed by the New York-based Rosoff Company. Once an area with a high rate of tuberculosis, it was known as the city's "lung blocks." Television's Hill's 1,319 foot, visually ubiquitous transmission tower soars out of the distant horizon. Mayor Thomas D'Alesandro, who approved its construction in 1956, called the project "big-league and worthy," sentiments echoed by viewers (some in Pennsylvania and Delaware) who marveled at the improved reception they received from their black and white Philcos and Zeniths.

MENCKEN SHOPPED HERE (PROBABLY): This was the 1600 block of W. Baltimore Street when H.L. Mencken lived in the neighborhood (in the 1500 block of Hollins Street) and much of Franklin Square's blue-collar, working class was still intact. At least 11 businesses thrived in these circa 1870s row houses on this block through the 1920s and 1930s. Who remembers Labovitz Drugs, Culotta's Confectionery, Yates Jewelers, Lord Baltimore Cleaners, Schlossburg Women's Wear? Who would admit it? The streetcar is either the number 2 or 15. The domed building is the long-forgotten West End, a movie theatre built by John K. McIver in 1911. Never very popular, particularly in winter when patrons shivered in its heatless 500-seat auditorium, it was playing out its final years in the silent era of Buster Keaton, Ben Turpin, Norma Talmadge, Blanche Sweet, Gloria Swanson and a host of other period Hollywood heavyweights. The West End closed in 1923, probably because of competition from the Capital, which opened in 1920 down the street. In 1924 it became the Maryland-West Virginia regional headquarters for the Salvation Army. *Peale Museum*

CRUMBLING: Much of the row, typical of Franklin Square's decaying commercial corridor, was demolished in 1995 after years of sitting vacant and boarded. Save for the drug pushers and their clients, the liquor store was the block's sole surviving business in mid-1996. Long in decline since World War Two, Franklin Square through much of the 1980s appeared headed for an economic reversal via a "shopsteading" program and Stephen's Square, a mix of apartments and mom-and-pop storefronts in the 1500 block of W. Baltimore Street launched by Stephen Terry, a California-based developer. For $100, budding entrepreneurs set up shop in government-financed renovated and furnished storefronts. It was a bold and inspiring, if not noble venture that failed because of a shrinking population base, crime and problems with rehabbing the storefronts. Completed in 1987 and acquired by HUD two years later, Stephen's Square in summer 1996 went on the auction block. About the only thing that hasn't abandoned this poor, forsaken place is the Salvation Army, a symbol of stability and hope in a community desperate for both.

BLOOMING BOULEVARD: The late 19th century was a time of broad, verdant thoroughfares. Paris' Avenue de l'Imperatrice became the model for many that sprouted in American cities. Chicago had its 200-foot wide Drexel Boulevard, Cleveland its Euclid Avenue, Milwaukee its Prospect Avenue, Baltimore its Eutaw Place, Mt. Royal Avenue, Broadway and Fulton Avenues, the latter forming the western edge of West Baltimore's Sandtown-Winchester district. Municipal planners laid out Fulton's well-manicured median around 1875–1876, part of a city-wide plan to splotch patches of parkland around regularly paved, grid-patterned streets. The Frick (named for Frank Frick, streetcar line magnate and founder of Lyric Theatre) horsecar line (later consolidated into the Baltimore Traction Company) began its run on Fulton around 1876 and enhanced land values. Development like the almost spanking-new, Italianate-style rows pictured here soon followed. The view shows a Frick car (left) heading south past step-washers and stoop-sitters enjoying what appears to be, judging by the awnings, a pleasant, sunny day. *Maryland Historical Society*

WILTED BOULEVARD: The bloom came off the topiary median in the mid-1890s when the Baltimore Traction Company electrified their vehicles and laid track on top of it. Concrete replaced grass altogether sometime in the 1950s, a municipal "improvement" that only further detracted from the aesthetics of a street that declined steadily after World War Two. "If you want to see how a city rots, take a look at Fulton Avenue," wrote *News-Post* columnist Louis Azreal in the late 1940s. Azreal lambasted greedy white landlords for destroying the neighborhood by subdividing single family homes into apartment units for the purpose of exploiting black tenants "hard up for living space." Azreal's editorial came at a time when Fulton Avenue was a racial dividing line between blacks east of it and whites west of it. A decade later, this was a predominately black neighborhood that was beginning to absorb an influx of poorer residents as middle-class blacks moved to newer neighborhoods like Edmondson Village. Long in serious decline by the mid-1990s, Sandtown-Winchester was in the midst of an encouraging, though languid rehabilitation program involving city agencies and Habitat For Humanity, which rehabbed about 60 houses between 1989 and 1996. The Enterprise Foundation, founded by the late James Rouse, financed a portion of the construction. City agencies were rehabbing the swell-front homes at left (the swell-front additions were probably added in the 1890s) when the author took this view in May 1996, two months after the Schmoke administration announced plans to demolish 800 city houses, some of them in Sandtown-Winchester.

DRUID HILL PARK OR BUST! Police and a Hughes Company photographer were on the scene shortly after this bus, after being hit by another vehicle, crashed into an unoccupied 1401 Druid Hill Avenue. Although the bus driver escaped injury, two workmen that had been rehabbing the house were hospitalized from injuries sustained from flying bricks. Druid Hill Avenue accommodated two-way traffic in those days. The turreted building at right (southeast corner of McCulloh and Lafayette), designed by architect Alfred Mason, was the whites-only Western High School between 1895 and 1925. In 1929 it became Booker T. Washington, a middle school for black students in what had been a German and Irish neighborhood from around 1870 to the mid-1890s. Upton, as this West Baltimore district (taking its name from the 1838 Greek Revival country house on W. Lanvale Street) came to be known, absorbed a large black population, much of it relatively middle class, from South Baltimore and the district's surrounding alley houses. *Peale Museum*

BUSTED: Upton, squeezed within the northwest quadrant of Baltimore's ailing 44th Legislative District, suffers from high unemployment, high crime, a low rate of home ownership, etc.—the usual menu of social ills that's plagued Baltimore's inner-city neighborhoods for decades. The flight of middle-class black residents beginning in the 1950s left Upton by the 1990s an impoverished and dangerous place, where only a handful of longtime residents remained, some engaged in valiant efforts to take back streets turned mean from the drug trade. Shown is an arrest in progress, a common happening here as expressed by the insouciant young cyclist at left.

The gabled double house at center stood here from at least 1850 until the mid-1920s. George Washington never slept here but Robert E. Lee did as the guest of then owner Frederick W. Brune, a noted Baltimore attorney who purchased it in 1868. In 1920 the house belonged to the state, whose plans for an armory on the site never materialized. The circa 1900 Greek revival-style Provident Savings Bank, founded in 1886, was one of the bank's 12 branch offices in 1920. In 1948 Provident moved their Northern branch elsewhere, and this crease of a building hasn't gotten much use since. The late Victorian-era Royalton apartment building shown behind it featured space for residential units and medical offices. Anybody remember Dr. William Conrad Bode or dentist Walter Hutson? The latter practiced here through the 1950s. The trolley heading north on Maryland Avenue is either the number 10 or 25. *Peale Museum*

The Brune house came down in the mid to late 1920s to make room for the 254-stall North Avenue Market. Opened in 1928, the market served an area that remained stable and middle-class through the 1950s. A devastating fire in August 1968 closed it for six years. Reopened in 1974 amid a neighborhood in decline, it was never the same place. Instead of stalls, it housed large retail concerns like Rite Aid (shown) and McCrory's. The 17-story 1973 senior citizens home in back of Rite Aid was one of many built for Baltimore's elderly throughout the 1960s and 1970s. The old Royalton, boarded for about a decade, emerged in the late 1990s as one of the city's rarely heard inner-city housing success stories. The Royalton Baltimore Housing Limited Partnership, the building's owners, rehabbed it in 1994. The helpful staff at Edgewood Management informed the author that as of April 1998, the building's 13 apartment units were all occupied, most of them by the same low- to mid-level income tenants that moved there following the rehab. Plans to resurrect the padlocked old Provident, also a Royalton property, hinge on the company's success in finding a suitable tenant.

Mt. Royal Terrace was the eastern-most boundary of what had been "Mount Royal," a 320 acre estate acquired in 1726 by Jonathan Hansen, a Pennsylvania Quaker. In the late 18th century, Hansen's heirs deeded much of the property to Samuel Birkhead, whose heirs in turn sold large tracts of it for sub-division after the Civil War. The homes at left were built around the time of the 1888 annexation, a time when real estate transactions doubled and people with means acquired property near Druid Hill Park. Fronting the then rural Jones Falls stream valley and developing Peabody Heights (forerunner of Charles Village) beyond, these were homes with a view. At center (on hill) is Druid Lake Tower, a power station overlooking the reservoir. *Pratt*

A historical preservation district since 1976, Mt. Royal Terrace became a labor of love for city-loving Baltimoreans with an appreciation for high porches (even though traffic whooshing by on the JFX had destroyed the once quiet, bucolic view of the Jones Falls stream valley), Queen Ann ornateness and the fortitude to enjoy it all while living on the edge of a war zone. Fortitude has its limits, however, as the author learned when he returned to inspect these houses in late 1997 and saw many of them boarded and tagged with auction signs.

From 1935 through 1938, Potts and Callahan construction crews were busy building the 29th Street Bridge. A WPA project costing $573,000, the 1,375 foot span would relieve traffic congestion on major city arteries like Howard Street and North Avenue and link Remington (in background), once a mill village, with what became known as Reservoir Hill. The bridge also made commuting easier for women textile workers, many of them migrants from Appalachia who during World War Two lived around Linden Avenue and worked in Hampden and Woodberry. The church, Keen Memorial, dates from the 1880s. At far left is the newly-completed, 290-bed United States Marine Hospital; at the time, it was the second largest marine hospital in the country. *Pratt*

(Continued on the following 2 pages)

10/30/3Y - 29TH STREET BRIDGE.   LEZPOLD PHOTO

Integrated in the 1960s into the JFX arterial system, the bridge spans what was once known as a sort of great divide between various racial and ethnic groups. First Jews, then Afro-Americans west of it lived apart from the predominately white Christian population of Remington and Hamden-Woodberry to the east. With integration, most notably in Remington, the symbolism has worn thin. The Marine Hospital, more recently known as Wyman Park Medical Center, was incorporated into the Johns Hopkins Health System. The 1974 Wyman House (far right) senior citizens complex looms conspicuous on a skyline that's changed little in 60 years.

Harford Road Looking North from Homestead Street

1911

1995

The city's third expansion in 1888 enveloped 19th century country estates like "Mondawmin" on the northwestern frontier and those contiguous to this northeastern view—"Cold Stream," "Homestead," "Montebello" and "Clifton." Here, a still unpaved Harford Avenue (tracks belong to the United Railways' #19 line), once a stagecoach line charted in 1816 as the Baltimore and Harford Turnpike, winds through the city's still rural suburban northeast quadrant. The area was not without some high-density residential settlement—rows of brick, post-Civil War homes stood just west of here, financed by Horace Abbott and Robert Gorsuch, Jr., two of the area's 19th century estate lords/speculators—but substantial rowhouse development would not commence until the late teens. The city had already purchased Johns Hopkins' "Clifton," (immediate right) and John W. Garrett's "Montebello," the eastern boundary of its spacious grounds extending to Harford Road. The former became a municipal park, the latter a grid-patterned, early 20th-century, middle-class neighborhood of daylight type row homes built by, among others, Frank Novak and E.J. Gallagher. Harford Road would become by the mid-1920s a paved, increasingly busy thoroughfare of streetcars and automobiles. *Pratt*

Beginning in the late 1970s, with the City Fair and its emphasis on neighborhood cohesiveness in full swing, many Baltimore neighborhoods that lacked a specific moniker tagged themselves with names indigenous to their past. This district became Coldstream, Homestead, Montebello, echoing the estates and the families ("Cold Stream" belonged to the Pattersons, "Homestead" to the Gorsuchs) that occupied them for much of the 19th century. Remnants from the early post-estate era include the old Harford Theatre (white building at left), which opened in 1916, closed in 1960, reopened in 1962 as an art theatre, then closed for good in 1963; it has since become a church. The old Harford's fortunes reflect the neighborhood's socio-economic decline since the 1960s. Up to the mid-1950s, the block between Homestead and Gorsuch claimed, including the theatre, a pharmacy, tailor shop, dentist's office and two confectioneries. Except for a liquor store/pharmacy (northwestern corner of Harford and Gorsuch), carryout and laundromat, this block by the mid-1990s was devoid of commercial interests. From this angle, Clifton Park looks much as it did in 1911.

(Full size photographs follow)

MARCH-29-11
HARFORD-AVE
OF HOMESTEAD-ST

HARFORD ROAD LOOKING NORTH FROM HOMESTEAD STREET, 1911

AT THE CROSSROADS: What became the commercial hub of Hamilton still looked like a rural crossroads in 1910, nine years before Hamilton's annexation to Baltimore City. The building shown housed the post office and probably a general store as well. In Bromley's 1915 Atlas of Baltimore County, Hamilton appears as a place in transition, with the multi-acre estates of the Reads, Gebbs, Sommers, Christophers, McAllisters and other area families surrounded by budding subdivisions like Altona Park, Hamilton Park and Echodale Terrace. Not really a trolley suburb in the tradition of Roland Park or Walbrook, Hamilton evolved slowly from a patch-quilt of 19th century farms and estates. Chugging along through the teens like the tin lizzie shown at left, it accelerated after 1920, its growth fueled by bigger, faster automobiles, municipal road-paving projects and real estate speculators prescient enough to cash in. *Peale Museum*

SATURDAY ROUNDS: "Hamilton will never be a shopping center but a place for shopping," merchant Warren Lakein told the author. The district in 1996 was not what it was in 1960, when Young's Mens and Boys Shop, S.S. Kresge, Wilkens Seafood House, Goldenberg's and the Arcade Theatre thrived here. Nevertheless, Main Street was alive and reasonably well, Lakein said—in spite of, perhaps even because of, The Mall. Retail concerns like Lakein's Jewelers and Camera Mart give quick, personalized service. The Signet Bank building dates from about 1920; originally the Hamilton Bank, it became Union Trust of Maryland in the mid-1920s.

3100 BLOCK OF GREENMOUNT AVENUE LOOKING NORTH, CIRCA 1890

When the old #8 trolley last rolled through Waverly in November 1963, Main Street's 19th century buildings had long been refitted with newer commercial wardrobes like the one draped over the old Sinclair place (Magic Mens Wear since 1977). Main Street's economic health has ebbed and flowed since then, hurt by middle-class flight and the Orioles' leap to Camden Yards (the overflow from Memorial Stadium was an important source of revenue to some Waverly businesses), helped by a shrunken but loyal middle-class determined to stay put, bus riders transferring at Greenmount Avenue and 33rd Street, (the second busiest transfer point in the city) and hard-working Korean, Chinese, Pakastani and Nigerian merchants providing essential goods and services.

CIRCA 1890 (LEFT): This was Waverly's Main Street near century's end—unpaved, unhurried and still the center of village life when village life included trips to the blacksmith and carriage builder. Founded in 1866 and originally known as Huntington, Waverly, like other suburban villages, grew steadily in the 1870s after horse car lines (the Peabody Heights and Waverly Horse Railway in Waverly's case) made them more accessible to Baltimore City. The photo shows no evidence of cable (save for the telephone wires) over what was then the York Turnpike, a sure sign that electric vehicles had not yet arrived. They finally did in April 1893, when Nelson Perin launched his Union Passenger Railway. Electrified mass transit stimulated massive strip development which in turn blurred lines of demarcation between 19th century villages like Waverly and Govanstown. The four-story, mid-19th century building with mansard roof, located just north of Merryman's Lane, belonged to the Sinclair's, one of the village's first families. *Peale Museum*

ELITE STREET: A decade before, it was known as Merryman's Lane, a rural thoroughfare connecting two turnpikes (Falls and York Roads) surrounded by 19th century country estates. In 1908 it became this—a classy conduit for tony North Baltimore's "green wedge," home to the city's "blue book" brigade, then flocking to burgeoning Roland Park and Guilford. Johns Hopkins University was the catalyst; in 1902 the school purchased for its permanent campus one of those country estates, "Homewood," plus additional property that later became Wyman Park ("Homewood" was sold by the Wyman family). Merryman's Lane became University Parkway, a boulevard confluent to the "green wedge" and the men who designed and developed it: Frederick Law Olmsted, the Boston landscape engineer under hire to study the Homewood area; Edward H. Bouton, president of the Roland Park Company; Edward L. Cotter, developer whose work conformed to Olmstead's landscaping scheme. Soon, the houses seen here just east of the #29 trolley line would give way to mid- and high-rise apartment buildings, housing tenants with names like Abell and Primrose, Chatterley and Van Sant. Note Greek revival-style First Church of Christ Scientist just north of Canterbury Road; built in 1913, it was constructed of white marble from Beaver Dam quarries. *Sun File Photo*

HIGH-RISE ROW: The 10-story, Wyatt and Nolting-designed 100 West University apartment building claimed the turreted Queen Ann Victorian house (the house appears in the 1877 Hopkins Atlas of the area) shown in earlier view. Built in the late 1920s, it was one of the first of the exclusive high-rises to grace the street from Calvert Street to Roland Avenue. Shown here, looking north, are The Broadview (1951), Hopkins House (1967) and The Carlyle (1965). The 1989 11-story Colonnade (foreground), part office complex, condo and hotel, is also home to the 5-star Polo Grill, scene of many a power meal among the city's movers and shakers and a hotspot for social-ites (and wannabees) of all races and creeds. The Colonnade spiced the staid boulevard with a certain swank and nouveau panache while respecting the architectural integrity of its neighbors. In scale and form, it has much in common with the solid, 1920s-era adjacent Northway (not shown). Leo J. D'Aleo, the building's principal architect, described his work as a "contemporary building using traditional forms." High-rise apartments facing Homewood Field have for decades afforded residents an added fringe benefit: Bird's-eye views of Bluejay lacrosse and football games.

WALBROOK JUNCTION, 25 JUNE 1927

WALBROOK JUNCTION

25 June 1927

PAS DE DEUX: Back in the 1920s, the junction's roundabout proved ideal for staging "streetcar ballets," a popular outdoor theatrical art form unique to the region. Actually, the "dance" is just an illusion created by the photographer who caught this motorman, his rider and an indifferent audience in the act of being themselves. On this particular day, Baltimoreans, like the rest of the world, were still reading about "lucky Lindy" and his derring-do over the Atlantic. Temperatures hovered in the mid to upper 70s, a welcome relief for parents and their offspring walking in a baby parade in Druid Hill Park to benefit the "Babies Hot Weather Fund." The U.S. Department of Labor, reported the day's edition of the *Baltimore News*, found that Baltimore led the nation's major cities in percentage of single family homes per family units built.

Some of those homes, among the city's largest, could be found in Walbrook, once the antebellum estate of Galloway Cheston (located at what is now Hilton Street and Walbrook Avenue) and

another multi-acre spread called Highland Park. Enter in 1870 developer Charles G. Wilson, president of the Chesapeake, Livingston and Franklin Building Associations. Wilson and his partners saw profit to be made by turning the place into a rural resort. They cut through some streets, built in 1874 a sprawling hotel, installed a horse-drawn railway and even laid down a half-mile boardwalk eastward to the Western Maryland Railway. But it didn't work, probably because of inadequate transportation. Ultimately, it took the electrified North Avenue Railway (forerunner of the Walbrook, Gwynn Oak & Pohatan Railway) in 1889 to rouse Walbrook from its drowsy, 19th century ruralness.

By the early 1890s, the place already had a Main Street, North Avenue, which Wilson et al had opened to 10th Street (now Ellamont Street). A secondary commercial area bounded by Clifton Avenue (rear of station house), Dennison Street and Windsor Mill Road (foreground) developed around the combination 1894 confectionery and station house shown here. Cannatella's shoe repair at 3409 Clifton (visible in background) shared the block with the Garrison Grill, Lexington Hardware and the Suburban Restaurant. The popular Blue Parrott Tea Room (later to become the Blue Astor Tea Room) fronted on Garrison Boulevard (left), a few doors north of Fibus Drug Store. Three streetcar lines, numbers 4, 13, 31, converged here, a sort of suburban grand central set amid sprawling Queen Anne-style homes parked on spacious lawns viewed from wrap-around porches, where rounds of chitchat filled warm evenings in the days before electronic entertainment. Automobiles like the one seen at left pulling onto Bloomingdale Road from Garrison Boulevard, would soon derail the vehicle that had jump-started Walbrook and other trolley suburbs like Windsor Hills and Forest Park. *Author's collection*

WALBROOK JUNCTION

1996

MOTOWN CONNECTION: For many baby-boomers who grew up here in the mid-1960s, Walbrook and Shorty Long's 1966 rhythmic Motown opus, *Function At The Junctio*n, are forever bound. Many first heard it tuned in to WEBB radio, then one of three local R&B or "soul" stations that in 1969 was purchased by Soul Brother Number One himself, James Brown. From a glass-enclosed broadcast booth at Clifton and Dennison Streets, the station's deejays spun the records and did their verbal shtick to the delight of passersby. Every day was a function at the junction. Then Brown went bankrupt and WEBB in 1984 moved (it folded in 1992) from the junction, already in transition from its trolley-era guise.

Walbrook Plaza, financed by two Baltimore physicians and grants from the community block grant program, added more retail space. Opened in May 1980, the shopping center, according to community activists, helped revitalize a Walbrook plagued by

crime and declining property values. Other changes followed: The station house, rebuilt of brick in 1943, disappeared in 1985, and along with it the venerated Blue Boy carry-out (luncheon at the junction often meant takeout from the Blue Boy) which operated from the station. The city's "Walbrook Street improvements" project, launched May 1983 and completed the following April, routed Oval Drive (foreground) over the old trolley roundabout. Even the southern end of Windsor Mill Road disappeared—buried, is more accurate, under the 1987 Walbrook Professional Building and its parking lot. The circa 1920 commercial building at right is the most prominent landmark, the only visible landmark save for the renovated commercial strip on Clifton, linking the 1996 junction with its 1927 predecessor. Not shown are the blocks of townhouses that began in the 1980s to replace Walbrook's older, decrepit housing stock.

(Full size photographs follow)

WALBROOK JUNCTION, 1996

LIBERTY HEIGHTS AND GARRISON BOULEVARD, 1937

(Narrative follows)

LIBERTY HEIGHTS AND GARRISON BOULEVARD

1937 Leafy, shaded Forest Park, the suburban dream of rowhouse dwellers seeking big, detached houses with lawns ideal for informal games of football and soccer, emerged in the 1890s from the flat fields of the Vickers, Slingluff and Gittings estates. Liberty and Garrison, a 19th century rural crossroads, became the area's commercial hub. The hacienda-style strip facing Liberty (odd side of the 3800 block), probably dating from 1915–1920, looked like this in 1937, the year former vice-president Spiro T. Agnew graduated (February '37) from Forest Park High School. It's likely that Agnew and his buddies, like other generations of Forest Park students before and since, snacked and schmoozed at the soda fountain in Read's drug store. If not there, then at Shure's Drug Store down the street at 3801 Liberty. S.S. Kresge was on the strip then, along with Wagner's, Martha Washington Candies, Lambros Restaurant and Confectionery (shown), the Arundel Ice Cream parlor, Liberty Hardware, Lewis' Deli and other businesses that made Forest Park a self-contained community in an era when people didn't travel as far as they do today.

1994 Cosmetically, the strip appears caught in a time warp, wearing the same facade it did 60 years ago, a facade the Liberty-Garrison Shopping Center Corporation (offshoot of the Greater Northwest Baltimore Community Coalition) hopes to renovate in 1998 if their requested $1 million block grant loan comes through. A $500,000 block grant loan in 1995 enabled the Corporation to finally repair the strip's leaky roofs. The strip claimed nine businesses in the late 1990s (T.P. Electronics, Garrison Hardware, Unisex Fashions, Pizza Boli's among them), down from 19 during the Depression year of 1937. In 1977, long after the relatively innocent days of drug store soda fountains, Rite Aid bought Read's and moved in the late 1980s a block south on Liberty's north side, while its old building enjoyed a brief run as a video store. Jim Parker's Lounge (formerly Lambros) might be Forest Park's greatest post-Eisenhower era commercial success story. Opened in 1966 by ex-Baltimore Colt Jim Parker, it continued to thrive into the 1990s. Like many suburban Baltimore neighborhoods from the late 1950s through the 1960s, Forest Park did a racial flip-flop, going from predominately white to black in less than a decade. In turn, that first generation of black middle-class residents, beginning in the 1970s, migrated out toward the northwest suburbs themselves, leaving behind a Forest Park that declined and evolved into a socio-economic hybrid of stable, middle-class home owners and impoverished transients, many of whom were no strangers to the criminal justice system. Long before the author snapped this view, Garrison and Liberty had earned a reputation as an open market for—in law enforcement parlance—controlled dangerous substances and related paraphernalia.

5100 BLOCK OF PARK HEIGHTS AVENUE LOOKING NORTH TOWARD BELVEDERE

1920

HORSE TOWN: Rutted and unpaved, Pimlico's Main Street in 1920 resembled a Western frontier town. Even sidewalks, as the photo reveals, arrived relatively late. A sparsely settled village surrounded by farmland and rural retreats just a few years before, Pimlico, like Waverly, melded into the municipal urban fold via political annexation and mass transit/development. Affordable porch-front row houses ($2,500–$7,000) went up during the teens, and a burgeoning middle-class from the inner-city moved out to buy them. Pimlico's business district started to take shape around 1910 when the Suburban Amusement and Development Co., led by Morris H. Wolfe, George Flint and Benjamin Beck, began buying property for commercial use. The Pimlico Theatre, shown at left, was one of Suburban's first projects. Designed by architect John R. Forsyth, it opened in 1914, the year Baltimore-born, cinematic heart-throb Francis X. Bushman, who would star in the silent *Ben Hur* 12 years later, won *The Ladies' World* Hero Contest. In ten years, not counting the movie, more than 15 businesses would be operating in the 5100 block, most of them on the street's even side. The trolley (right) is most likely a United Railway's #5 car, a descendant of the horse cars that began running along Park Heights Avenue at "irregular intervals" in 1873, the year of the first Preakness.

An ethnically diverse, stable, lower middle-class to middle-class neighborhood through the 1950s, Pimlico also carried a somewhat tough-guy reputation. Wise guys, drapes, goodfellas, whatever the locals called them, Pimlico seemed to attract an inordinate number, perhaps because of its track. Like Forest Park, Pimlico experienced dramatic racial turnover in the 1960s. Residents in pursuit of a "greater" American Dream, both black and white, used it as a springboard into upper Park Heights and beyond. *Peale Museum*

1996

EASY MONEY: The woman that wandered in front of the author's lens, openly counting a stack of bills, appeared oblivious to the dangers of Pimlico's mean streets in the 1990s. The neighborhood where "police calls are rare," as a November 1950 *Evening Sun* community profile reported, had become in 20 years the headline for an August 1970 *News American* profile: "Fear Is Key Word In Vocabulary of Pimlico People." A quarter century later, with street crime even worse, Pimlico headed toward the new millennium as another sad chapter in Baltimore's lengthening book of declining city neighborhoods. Its commercial heart still beat, though irregularly, and inside an ailing body of declining property values and homes falling into abandonment and disrepair. The 5100 block, though structurally intact, was plagued with vacant retail space, including the old Pimlico Theatre. After its last picture show (probably "The Redhead and the Cowboy" starring Rhonda Flemming, 8 September 1952), Read's Drugs occupied the space between 1953–1977. Its last tenant, Mega Value Mall, closed in the early 1990s. As of late 1997 the building sat vacant and padlocked, a tragic reflection of the area it once served. But there was still the track and its world-famous Preakness.

(Full size photographs follow)

ON THE FAST TRACK: Mt. Washington in 1900 was both a trolley and railroad suburb, served by the Northern Central Railroad and the newly-consolidated (as of March 1899) United Railways and Electric Company of Baltimore. Overhead is the United Railways' steel trestle, installed in 1897 to ferry its cars over the Jones Falls from Falls Road to Sulgrave Avenue (then North Avenue). The Northern Central was founded in 1854 (consolidated from the Baltimore and Susquehanna and other lines), the same year a real estate speculator named George Gelbach founded Mt. Washington as a commuter suburb, arguably Baltimore's first, for the city's well-to-do merchant class. Gelbach's ads touted the Northern Central's efficiency, and rightfully so: By the mid-1880s, 16 trains daily were available to Mt. Washington commuters, nearly 20 by 1900. The mid-1870s, board-and-batten design station house (left of tracks) in this northbound view also served as living quarters for the railroad agent. Washingtonville, a blue-collar hamlet built in the early 1800s to house mill workers, stood just east of here, on the "other side of the tracks." *Author's collection*

BACK TO THE FUTURE: While Mt. Washington maintained its status as a community of high achievers, the fortunes of the Northern Central, like other railroads, declined through the 20th century. From a peak of 27 trains daily each way (1904), the "Parkton local" by the late 1950s (then under the Pennsylvania Railroad) offered just three trains each way; in 1959 the line ceased passenger service altogether. In 1968 a private, locally-based firm tore down the old station house (a weekend sneak-attack is the way some remember it) before preservationists could mount an effective strategy to save it. Environmental activists from Mt. Washington and other communities along the old NCRR right-of-way (Parkton, Ruxton, etc.) did stage a vigorous protest against the proposed electric Light Rail system, insisting it would invite littering and vandalism. Thus far it hasn't. Light Rail (the state purchased the right-of-way in 1990 from Conrail) proved efficient and, for the most part, environment-friendly from the time it opened in spring 1992. Over 20 trains daily served Mt. Washington in the mid-1990s, and over 24,000 riders daily were using the system by early 1998, up from 5,000 in 1992.

WAITING FOR THE TRIPPER: George Webb's Northern Electric Railway installed this station house about the same time the company's trestle was completed. A real estate/transportation tycoon who later dabbled in motion picture technology, Webb was instrumental in the chesslike political and financial maneuvering that consolidated his company and other trolley lines into the United Railways system. Webb's cars, among the fastest of any Baltimore line, helped turn Mt. Washington from primarily a summer resort into a year-round commuting suburb, a process the automobile would complete in a decade or so, bringing to a close the era when wooden footbridges spanned streams like Western Run and horse-driven carriages rolled along muddy, unpaved streets like Sulgrave Avenue. Shown just left of the trestle (dismantled in 1927 after the concrete viaduct was completed) is the roof of James Hamilton's general store. *Author's collection*

GONE TO THE DOGS: The old waiting station got recycled into a drug store and then a confectionery before veterinarian Bruce Hornstein bought the building and established a thriving practice here in 1964. Mt. Washington's big homes and lawns made for a high ratio of pet ownership (big dogs are especially plentiful), Dr. Hornstein figured, and he was right. His business took off, necessitating the need for the circa 1970 twin addition. He practiced here for 32 years and saw over 60 of his employees become vets themselves. The A-framed building is the latest addition to the Mt. Washington Tavern (originally the home of Hamilton's store), a favorite jock/preppie hangout created in 1979 by two Gilman grads. They renovated what was once a seedy, blue-collar neighborhood pub into one of Mt. Washington Village's most successful enterprises. Like the bygone Pimlico Hotel before it, The Tavern became a staple among northwest Baltimore eateries, drawing patrons from other areas.

ENDANGERED SPECIES: A mile past the Mt. Washington waiting station, passengers riding the United Railways' Pikesville-bound route saw this pastoral slice of Baltimore County off to their left. The house on hill dates from the 1880s and belonged to the Hoopers, a family associated with Baltimore's lucrative cotton duck industry. The covered bridge is one of at least six that existed in Baltimore County (there were once over 52 in Maryland) at the turn of the century. Covered bridges in America date from 1804, the year Timothy Palmer built the Schuylkill Permanent Bridge in Philadelphia. Maryland got its first covered bridge 13 years later, the huge 4,170-foot, 18-arch structure that spanned the Susquehanna River at Rock Run. The specimen shown here probably dates from the period 1860–1890, covered bridge-building's golden age, and appears to have vanished in history's proverbial dust bin. With the exception of one brief mention in a book of personal reminiscences, the bridge is conspicuous by its absence in articles the author researched on covered bridges in Maryland and Baltimore County. *Author's collection*

WATER UNDER THE BRIDGE: A young couple strolls north on a bridge designed for the realities of 20th century travel, not the romanticism associated with covered bridges. Relics of a nation of small towns and farms, they died of attrition, many of them falling victim to state and county highway departments, bureaucracies not known for their sentimentalism. Maryland had but 17 left in 1937, eight in 1968, three as of 1995, and only one of them was in Baltimore County (at Jericho). The Pimlico Road bridge probably vanished sometime between 1900 and 1918, the year Baltimore City absorbed Mt. Washington and other northwest suburbs. This mid-1950s concrete span isn't as cute, but it gets the job done, bearing an increasingly heavy load of automobile traffic. Under the bridge, one can find concrete abutments (they supported the tracks), artifacts from the trolley era that ended for Mt. Washington in the late 1940s. Just beyond here, apartment buildings and single homes occupy what in 1900 was a barren hillside. The old Hooper place still stands off of what became Rusk Avenue. Even older is the stone house at right, an area landmark dating from the early 1800s that some believe was once used by Charles Carroll for a hunting lodge.

JONES FALLS EXPRESSWAY LOOKING SOUTH AT CITY LINE, 2 NOVEMBER 1962

(Narrative follows)

Jones Falls Expressway Looking South At City Line

2 November 1962

1996

FANFARE FOR THE COMMUTING MAN: Roaring through what was once a placid stream valley, the JFX, planned a decade before, opened ceremoniously on the unseasonably chilly morning of 2 November 1962 (an era began as another was ending; almost one year later to the day, 3 November 1963, the #8 streetcar would make its final run). In sight of the Kelly Ave. bridge and Mt. Washington Village, Governor J. Millard Tawes and Mayor J. Harold Grady cut the ribbon with six foot scissors and gave speeches, praising the financial cooperation between Baltimore City and Baltimore County, calling the $55,000,000, nine mile (from downtown to the Baltimore beltway which opened 1 July 1962) thoroughfare a great boost for business and vital to the downtown revitalization effort. Bernard L. Werner, the city's director of public works, said the JFX, theoretically, could carry 200,000 vehicles daily, a far cry from the 40,000 vehicles daily that actually rolled over it during its first year. Meanwhile, commuters back in the heady days of the New Frontier were amazed: Barring mishaps, they could reach the Beltway from City Hall in 15 minutes. Wow! *Maryland Historical Society*

OUTBOUND: An ongoing migration to suburbia and women entering the workforce en masse nudged the JFX's ADT (average daily traffic) upward from its 1963 tally: 55,000 vehicles daily in 1968, 60,000 in 1977, 90,000 in 1985, a total that stood a decade later as Light Rail and the metro combined to ease congestion on the JFX and secondary routes. More telling is the substantial increase in the city line to 695 commute—from 24,000 to 74,500 vehicles daily between 1963–1995—reflecting suburbia's gain in jobs (under construction in background is USF&G's 850-space parking garage to serve their new Mt. Washington campus) as well as population and Baltimore's loss of both. In 1963 935,000 people lived in Baltimore City. In early 1998 only 657,000 (the city lost 79,000 residents between 1990–1998 alone!) did. In 1963 the classic suburb (or municipal fringe) to downtown and back commuting pattern was still the norm. By the mid-1990s more commuters were going from suburb to suburb, a pattern that influenced the State Highway Administration to add more lanes (an eight lane beltway from Reisterstown Road to the I-83 south exit is scheduled for completion in fall 1998) to the heavily congested, ever-widening beltway.

Jones Falls Expressway Looking South At City Line *(continued)*

As its planners predicted, the JFX forged a vital link between downtown Baltimore, suburban Baltimore County and what in the early 1960s was considered exurbia—the surrounding counties, then mostly rural. In the late 1990s that link was no less vital. On weekends, young partiers filled up the ubiquitous watering holes in Canton and Fells Point, tourists promenaded at Harborplace, Orioles fans cheered on Cal Ripken et al at Camden Yards, Ravens fans cheered on their new NFL football team in their new stadium at Camden Yards. Many of those revelers cruised into town via the JFX, driving their jeeps and minivans and SUVs from their suburban sanctums in Baltimore, Carroll and Harford counties and the growing suburban areas just north of the Mason-Dixon line. Baltimore City, once a place close to a million people called home, had become to over a million people little more than a weekend playground . . . a nice place to visit—but not such a nice place to live.

"Commuters give the city its tidal restlessness; natives give it solidity and continuity; but the settlers give it passion," wrote E.B. White in 1949. With more and more passion being drained from Baltimore each year, we have to wonder: Will city residents continue to stampede out to the counties, or will there be a leveling off, perhaps even a return in appreciable numbers of middle and upper-middle income families to city neighborhoods long abandoned?

A continuance of present demographic trends would mean a more advanced scenario of what we have today: neighborhoods turned into ghost towns, blocks of two or three rowhomes sans the rows ("missing teeth effect"), open air drug markets, depressed commercial strips and a pyramid-shaped socio-economic structure supporting the Uptons, Sandtown-Winchesters and Pimlicos at one end, the Guilfords, Ashburtons and Roland Parks at the other. Not a pretty forecast.

Few expect a dramatic reversal of the last half century—a return to the city by hundreds of thousands. There's nothing to indicate it will ever happen, certainly not in the next couple decades. The harsh realities of urban life in Baltimore City 1998 don't bode well for a resuscitated Howard and Lexington drawing throngs of Christmas shoppers or a safe, revitalized Pimlico. Still, it's fun to dream; dreams are the stuff of ideas, and ideas, good ones, have been known to turn things around.

Whatever its future, Baltimore, like other cities, like other places, will, for better or worse, continue to evolve, reinvent and redefine itself. Parts of the city will die as other parts are reborn. And photographers will continue to record it all from atop the usual lookouts (Federal Hill, Shot Tower, First and Franklin Presbyterian Church), freezing time in the fluid, frenzied, endless dance of change.

FALLS ROAD

Before the JFX, commuters took horse-and-buggy-era routes like Falls Road to travel to and from town. The road was built as a turnpike in 1810, the same year the Washington Manufacturing Company began producing cotton just two blocks south of the intersection pictured here. In 1930 the once Hooper-owned old cotton duck mill was turning out nuts and bolts (Hooper sold his Mt. Washington plant to Maryland Nut and Bolt Company in 1923), providing jobs for area residents. This semi-rural view sits just north of what had been Baltimore County until the city's last municipal expansion in 1918. The "new" city-county line made for divided loyalties among the neighborhood's grade-school youngsters: City kids attended Mt. Washington's school, while the county kids headed north to the Bare Hills school. Note the workman on the porch roof at the right and the sign posting a seven-acre lot for sale, part of what had once been the L. Thompson estate. This corner was the future site of the Lake Falls Drive-In, the first of the intersection's burger and pizza outposts. The building at the left, owned by the same family since the Civil War, has been a food store of one kind or another since the days when farmers hauled their goods into Baltimore by wagon train. In the 1930s this building housed the Rehbeins grocery store; Lacey's, a produce concern, operated here for the better part of the 1990s; and Bonjour, a bakery, opened here in late 1998. Commercial encroachment beginning in the late 1970s would claim the corner house and others further south on the east side of Falls Road. *Peale Museum*

Jaded commuters tired of JFX backups take Falls Road as a scenic, less stressful alternative to and from the city. In the late 1990s close to 12,000 vehicles passed this intersection daily, appreciably less than the 90,000 or so registered on the JFX's ADT. The commercialization is evident: Pepe's opened circa 1974 where the Lake Falls Drive-In used to be and Wawa opened about 1989. Etches, a cosmetic boutique, opened in 1997 in the 1980 Dutch Colonial-style house (6071 Falls Road) at the right, once field offices for Long and Foster realtors. Its predecessor sat vacant for over a decade before it came down in the late 1970s. Sunporch Antiques, Bonjour's next-door neighbor, opened in 1994 as an almost totally restored 6072 Falls Road. Barely visible at the left is the Mackenzie-managed Lake Falls Village, a retail and office complex completed in 1981. Attrition, not the village, took the two framed, shingled houses shown in the 1930 view, and 6078 Falls Road, home to generations of Newbars, was razed in the 1960s. Number 6076, or at least what was left of it, came down in 1959. The story of the house's partial demise in 1958 by a runaway dump truck barreling down from Lake Avenue is legendary among long-time area residents: Neighbors say the truck hit just as an elderly resident began shaving. Fittingly, only the Pahl family, who lived there at the time of the accident, can recall the accident's precise details. Pahl, Roche, Brookhart, Tormey, Imhoff, Hook—families that settled in the Lake Falls area early in the century, and in some cases even earlier, live there still.

African-American residential enclaves developed after the Civil War as former slaves and their relatives sought shelter in a racially segregated society. East Towson, Bare Hills, Kelly Avenue in Mt. Washington, and this stretch of Falls Road just north of Cold Spring Lane rep-

resent some of these enclaves. The photo fails to convey just how large this community was at one time; long before Poly-Western High School and the Village of Cross Keys arrived, the neighborhood claimed almost 50 houses, a church, and a meeting hall. Whatever happened to Ruth Bernice Hawkins, Sidney Henry, Franklin Jones, Lillian Avery, Theodore Clay, and John Bond, residents who once lived here? The tony Baltimore Country Club, within comfortable walking distance, might have served as a source of employment for some of the local residents. Persons working in the city could take the streetcar, a convenience dating back to the debut of the Falls Road Electric Railway in 1894. The Baltimore Address Telephone Directory does not list the block's even side (left) after June 1961, a sure sign that residents vacated their homes soon thereafter to make way for the mid-1960s Poly-Western High School complex. *Peale Museum*

The Poly-Western complex parking lot has defined this stretch of Falls Road more than 30 years. Little wonder that few remember or know what existed here for almost a century prior. The enclave's eastern half died a slower death, falling in piecemeal, house by house, to new development like the 120-bed Manor Care nursing facility (1997) at the right. Boswell Surveys, Inc. (right), a radon testing concern that has been here since the late 1980s, operates from a renovated 19th century house just out of view.

FALLS ROAD LOOKING NORTH FROM LAKE AVENUE, 20 FEBRUARY, 1930

224　4600–4700 BLOCK OF FALLS ROAD LOOKING NORTH, CIRCA 1925

4600–4700 BLOCK OF FALLS ROAD LOOKING NORTH, 1999

The view William H. Weaver captured in this classic photograph is another slice of 19th century Baltimore lost to the ages. The bridge crossed the Jones Falls at a northeast-southwest angle where the stream bent sharply eastward, its course forming a horseshoe-shaped pattern on its western bank. Belvidere Street, an important link between Baltimore and the country estates to the northeast, emptied into Greenmount Avenue at the entrance to Greenmount Cemetery. The E. Sachse & Company's remarkably detailed 1869 Bird's Eye View picture map rendered the bridge and its surroundings almost exactly as Weaver's view shows it—down to the rocks in the dam pool and the trees clumped around the southwest entrance. Oral histories of the area taken in the 1920s describe a summer and winter playground of swimming, ice-skating, and horseback riding. Built around 1820, the bridge was engineered to last—and it did, weathering the periodic flooding that destroyed other bridges spanning the Falls. It supported countless trips by countless wagon trains and might, with improvements, have taken on the first automobiles had it not been torn down in 1888. *Baltimore Sun File Photo*

Mr. Weaver would be hard-pressed to find the place he recorded for posterity on that day in 1874. The Falls runs underground, asphalt blankets what were once bridle paths and pastureland, and buildings stand where trees once grew. Ironically, it is the JFX, that six-lane concrete symbol of the automobile age, that provides the strongest link to Weaver's photograph. Note how it bulges eastward under Preston Street, following the ancient course of its namesake. Further east, the last remnant of Belvidere Street hangs off Greenmount Avenue, a half-block of asphalt to nowhere. The present bridge, a structural appendage of the JFX project, dates to 1959. Interestingly, the Belvidere was the only bridge in this location to accommodate vehicular traffic (earlier and later footbridges carried pedestrians over the Jones Falls and Fallsway) until city engineers extended Preston Street from Guilford Avenue. The heavy-duty iron 1936 Guilford Avenue bridge, shown rising above Preston Street, replaced another iron structure dating from 1879. Other area landmarks shown include the 1905 eight-story 218 Preston Street apartment building (left) and the 1897 Fallsway Building (center), a residential and industrial complex that originally housed Crown, Cork, and Seal, the bottle-top manufacturing giant.

BROADWAY FROM BALTIMORE STREET LOOKING SOUTH, CIRCA 1890

BROADWAY FROM BALTIMORE STREET LOOKING SOUTH, 1999

Broadway from Baltimore Street Looking South, circa 1890

Ropes put the broad in Broadway—ropes used in shipping were twisted by hand by rope-makers with the aid of a hand winch on the ropewalk that once stood at the center of this street below Baltimore Street. The walk and its industry required a street widening, allowing for pedestrian access. Market Street, as it was once called, became Broadway, famed for its exquisitely manicured squares, one for each block set between Baltimore Street and North Avenue. The one shown here looks all spruced up with newly planted trees, fresh cement, and shiny lawn urns. The horsecar (center) is a descendant of City Passenger's Red Line, inaugurated in 1859. Riders paid five cents for the service, which began at Broadway and Thames Street, turned west on Baltimore and rolled out to Smallwood Street, then West Baltimore's hinterland. The antebellum house at the left (1701 East Baltimore Street) is shown after its 1870s Victorian redo; period appurtenances included a mansard roof, bay windows, and New Orleans-style iron work. Its mansard-topped neighbor at the right (1645 East Baltimore Street) might also be a Victorianized affair; as late as 1870 a hipped-roofed two-story house stood here. John F. Hancock, "chemist and druggist," moved his pharmacy business from Baltimore and Caroline Streets to this corner in 1881. It is Hancock, according to one source, who might have financed the building's construction. As the sign notes, the house also accommodated dental offices. The steeple of Saint Patrick's Church and Fells Point Market can be seen in the distance. *Baltimore Sun File Photo*

Broadway from Baltimore Street Looking South, 1999

Broadway's southernmost square's latest landscaping includes a bricked surface bordered by wooden benches. The sign shown at the garden's edge (center) reads *Washington Hill,* an old name (taken from the Broadway medical hospital where Edgar Allan Poe died in 1849) revived by the city around 1972 for what became an urban renewal district. HUD money paid for the subsequent renovation into co-ops of 218 housing units in 90 buildings, including 1701 East Baltimore Street. Private funding renovated hundreds more during the Schaefer administration's halcyon days of urban homesteading. The Broadway Pharmacy (right), said to be Maryland's oldest pharmacy in operation, still thrives in this present age of chain-store monoliths like Rite Aid. Washington Hill, like its ancient corner apothecary, soldiers on amid a city losing a thousand residents a month.

BIBLIOGRAPHY

1. *America By Design*, Spiro Kostof, Oxford University Press 1987

2. *A Guide To Baltimore Architecture* (third edition), John Dorsey and James D. Dilts, Tidewater Publishers 1997

3. *A Stitch In Time*, Philip Kahn, Jr., Maryland Historical Society 1989

4. *Baltimore: A Not Too Serious History*, Letitia Stockett, Grace Gore Norman, 1936

5. *Baltimore's Cast Iron Buildings And Architectural Ironwork*, James Dilts and Catherine F. Black, Tidewater Publishers 1991

6. *Baltimore Deco*, S. Cucchiella, Maclay and Associates 1983

7. *Baltimore Harbor—A Picture History*, Robert C. Keith, Ocean World Publishing Company, Inc. 1982

8. *Baltimore—The Building Of An American City*, Sherry H. Olson, Johns Hopkins University Press 1980

9. *Baltimore—When She Was What She Used To Be, 1850–1930*, Marion E. Warren and Mame Warren, Johns Hopkins University Press 1983

10. *Bygone Baltimore*, Jacques Kelly, Donning Co. 1982

11. *Downtown, Inc.*, Bernard J. Frieden and Lynne B. Sagalyn, MIT Press

12. *Exit—A History Of Movies In Baltimore*, Robert Kirk Headley, Jr., Robert Kirk Headley, Jr. 1974

13. *Lost Baltimore Landmarks*, Carleton Jones, Maclay and Associates 1982

14. *Mount Vernon Place*, John Dorsey, Maclay & Associates, 1983

15. *North Baltimore—From Estate To Development*, Karen Lewand, Baltimore City Department of Planning and University of Baltimore 1989

16. *Peabody Heights To Charles Village*, Jacques Kelly, Equitable Trust Bank 1976

17. *The Baltimore Sun—1837–1987*, Harold A. Williams, Johns Hopkins University Press 1987

18. *The History Of Baltimore's Streetcars* (formerly *Who Made All Our Streetcars Go?*), Michael R. Farrell, Greenberg Publishing Co., Inc. 1992

19. *The Story Of The Northern Central Railway*, Robert L. Gunnarsson, Greenberg Publishing Co., Inc. 1991

20. *Those Old Placid Rows*, Natalie Shivers, Maclay and Associates 1981

21. *West Baltimore Neighborhoods*, Roderick N. Ryon, Institute For Publications Design, University Of Baltimore 1993

ACKNOWLEDGEMENTS

The author is indebted to many people for their invaluable assistance and contributions to this project:

Bruce Savadow, professional photographer and close friend, in addition to duplicating Pratt prints and developing film and contact sheets, took me through his own personal crash course on photography; if not for him, I'd still be trying to figure out how to load the camera.

Ervin Miller, my generous dad, kindly consented to lend me his Pentax K-1000 for as long as I needed it.

Peggy Mignini came through like the supportive, loving sister she's always been.

Bert Smith, professor at the University of Baltimore, and Margie Ann Bonnet, one of his students, worked up several cover designs as part of Ms. Bonnet's course work.

James D. Dilts, co-author of *A Guide To Baltimore Architecture*, kindly consented to write the Foreword to this book; he encouraged me throughout this project and was never too busy to answer questions or make suggestions.

Edward Gunts, *Sun* architecture critic, lent me his time and expertise whenever I called him.

Bennard Perlman, artist and teacher, tracked down information on the old Saint Paul Street Bridge.

William Guy Jr. provided information on 100 West University Parkway, of which he is co-owner.

Francis Schonowski, engineer for Baltimore City Bureau of Transportation, researched information on urban renewal projects for Walbrook and Madison Avenue.

Dr. Bruce Hornstein passed on historical and anecdotal information about the Mt. Washington Animal Medical Center.

R. Roland Brockmeyer supplied information on the chimney corner house (532 St. Paul Street); his law office is located there. Lillian Laird supplied additional information on the house and Enrico Liberti, the cabinet maker who occupied it for over 40 years; she is his daughter.

Bosley Tawney, sales manager for Parkway Holdings Ltd., supplied updates on Harbor View.

Michael Abrams, owner of the Abell Building, supplied updates on his building and the old loft district.

John Saunders and Stanley Zerden, presidents of the Liberty-Garrison Shopping Center Corporation and Oldtown Mall Merchants Association respectively, updated me on the commercial/economic developments in their neighborhoods.

Lenora Nast and Carleton Jones of the Historic Baltimore Society: Lenora encouraged me when I most needed encouraging and suggested ways to fund the project; Carleton imparted his vast knowledge of Baltimore history whenever I asked for it.

Middleton Evans, Baltimore photographer/author/publisher, was always helpful and patient when I needed advice.

Jeff Korman, John Sondheim, Lee Lears, Eva Slezak and other patient, helpful staff in the Pratt's Maryland Room provided research tips and liberal access to the Pratt's photo and directory files.

Sandra Levy and Nancy Opel, *Baltimore Sun* librarians, collected a number of *Sun* photos for me to choose from.

David Wallace, trustee of the First and Franklin Presbyterian Church, rounded up the Weaver, Machlachlan, and McCash steeple-view prints and lent me office space to sort them out.

Elaine Macklin, Resident Manager at Sutton Place since 1980, granted time for an interview and faxed a wealth of material.

Wendall Sutton, City Hall coordinator and his staff, Jimmy and Charlie, made possible my views from City Hall; Michael Eckhardt, manager at NationsBank Building, and Pearl Dreibelbis, his assistant, arranged for my panoramic views from the 34th floor; Walter Neighoff, Maintenance Manager for the Park Charles Building, arranged for my rooftop views of the Lexington Street mall; Al Melaragno of the city's maintenance department and members of his staff, William Frank and Ben Baylor, got me on top of the Baltimore Arts Tower; and Jamie Hunt, Public Relations Coordinator for Baltimore City Life Museums, climbed 215 feet of steps—on two occasions—so I could take views from the Shot Tower.

Averil Kadis, Chief of Public Relations for the Pratt Library, Mary Markey, photo curator for the Peale Museum, Jeff Goldman, photo curator for the Maryland Historical Society, Tom and John Beck (no relation), photo curators for University of Maryland Baltimore County, Marion Warren, author and historian, and Ann Calhoun, archivist for the Baltimore and Ohio Railroad Museum, offered me very generous discounts on user's fees.

Finally, I'd like to give special thanks to my wife, Nancy Yates-Miller, whose words and deeds, love and understanding encouraged and supported me throughout this project.

Library of Congress Cataloging-in-Publication Data

Miller, Mark B.
    Baltimore transitions : views of an American city in flux / by Mark B. Miller. — Rev. ed.
      p.   cm.
    Originally published : Baltimore, MD : Pridemark Press, 1998.
    Includes bibliographical references.
    ISBN 0-8018-6295-7 (alk. paper)
    1. Baltimore (Md.)—History Pictorial works.   2. Baltimore (Md.) Pictorial works.   I. Title.
F189.B157M55 2000
975.2′6′00222—dc21   99-42047